"Crum uncovers the Maker's fingerprints on our inner selves, reminding us that our self-worth is not lost, just waiting to be dusted off. This book, a guide to self-love, is filled with wisdom, humor, and invaluable insights that will empower you to live life with new-found confidence and authenticity."

—MARK BATTERSON, *New York Times* bestselling
author of *The Circle Maker*

"I started reading *Neighbor, Love Yourself* because the author asked me to; I finished reading it because I couldn't put it down. As one who has lost so many I love, I found that this book puts words to the truths I want to live out before forever begins."

—RACHEL WOJO, author of *One More Step* and *Pure Joy*

"Crum has done a great job of outlining applicable, hands-on ideas for how we can use our God-breathed wiring to improve our lives and the lives of others. He has deep reservoirs of wisdom, but he also tells a great story. One of his stories made my family snort-laugh over dinner as I read it to them, and when we finished laughing, we talked about the good, true things we learned in that same chapter. *Neighbor, Love Yourself* is that kind of book."

—KIMBERLY STUART, author and public speaker

"Bryan Crum and I have been talking about *Neighbor, Love Yourself* for a while now, and it's got all the pieces important to a great book. It has relatability, authenticity, and applicability. It will make you laugh. It will make you cry. It will make you think. *Neighbor, Love Yourself* has tools for helping you moving forward, and I really think you are going to like this book."

—BOB GOFF, *New York Times* bestselling author

"Bryan Crum has always had a gentle and witty way of telling the truth while encouraging me to seek God's direction in my life. In *Neighbor, Love Yourself,* he does just that. While reading about his real-life experiences, I can hear him urging us to love how God has uniquely and purposefully made us. God has big plans for us all . . . we just need to engage with his plans."

—NATE HARMON, lead pastor of Louisville
Baptist Temple, Louisville, Ohio

"God created in each of us a desire to know and be known by him. He equipped us with everything we need to live in a vibrant relationship with him. Unfortunately, our desire to know him often gets crushed by the busyness of our everyday lives, and we begin to doubt that we have anything within us that God can use. In *Neighbor, Love Yourself,* Bryan Crum helps us uncover the potential hidden deep within us. He weaves stories of lessons learned from those nearing the end of their lives to encourage us to make the most of the life we have. I highly recommend this enjoyable book to all who desire a deeper, more fulfilling relationship with Christ."

—DR. MARK MILIONI, president of Baptist Bible College

"You're holding an absolute treasure. If you struggle with self-compassion or wrestle to see yourself the way God sees you, this book is pure gold. You'll find your heart softened, your mind opened, your soul lifted. Crum pulls you in with his storytelling, hands you a precious souvenir to carry with you from each chapter, and points you in the direction of unending love."

—AMY SEIFFERT, Bible teacher and author of *Starved*
and *Grace Looks Amazing on You*

"I'm so proud of Bryan Crum and honored to have him as a member of my Writers Guild. *Neighbor, Love Yourself* is an important, potentially life-changing book, thoughtfully and poignantly rendered. The author's many stories transport us on a journey we all need to take."

—JERRY B. JENKINS

NEIGHBOR,
LOVE YOURSELF

NEIGHBOR, LOVE YOURSELF

DISCOVER YOUR VALUE, LIVE YOUR WORTH

Bryan Crum

Foreword by New York Times
bestselling author Bob Goff

WATERBROOK

A WaterBrook Trade Paperback Original

Copyright © 2024 by Bryan Crum
Foreword by Bob Goff copyright © 2024 by Penguin Random House LLC

All rights reserved.

Published in the United States by WaterBrook, an imprint of Random

House, a division of Penguin Random House LLC.

WATERBROOK and colophon are registered trademarks
of Penguin Random House LLC.

Quotes on pp. 33–34 are from *Stripey Bottom* by Bryan Crum, self-published
by the author in 2017, text copyright © 2017 by Bryan Crum,
illustrations copyright © 2017 by Jessica Flannery.

LIBRARY OF CONGRESS CATALOGING-IN-PUBLICATION DATA
Names: Crum, Bryan, author.
Title: Neighbor, love yourself : discover your value, live your worth /
Bryan Crum ; foreword by Bob Goff.
Description: Colorado Springs : WaterBrook, [2024] | Includes
bibliographical references.
Identifiers: LCCN 2023028624 | ISBN 9780593600993 (trade paperback) |
ISBN 9780593601006 (ebook)
Subjects: LCSH: Self-acceptance--Religious aspects--Christianity. |
Self-esteem--Religious aspects--Christianity.
Classification: LCC BV4647.S43 C78 2024 | DDC 248.4--dc23/eng/20231206
LC record available at https://lccn.loc.gov/2023028624

Printed in the United States of America on acid-free paper

waterbrookmultnomah.com

2 4 6 8 9 7 5 3 1

Book design by Caroline Cunningham

Most WaterBrook books are available at special quantity discounts for bulk purchase
for premiums, fundraising, and corporate and educational needs by organizations,
churches, and businesses. Special books or book excerpts also can be created to fit
specific needs. For details, contact specialmarketscms@penguinrandomhouse.com.

To Maggie and Casey,

who have made a story worth telling

FOREWORD

I love flying seaplanes. They come in handy for my wife, Sweet Maria, and me since they're the only way to get to one of the places we live. You've probably seen planes like this; they look like they have two canoes strapped to their feet in the places where wheels would normally be. I guess someone realized wheels don't work well in water and made the change.

Many of us are like seaplanes who have forgotten about our flying ability. Most of us have spent so much time floating on the water or tied to the dock that we've missed out on the great wealth in our wings. Seaplanes have value in the water, but if they remain there, they will never experience the heights and places they were meant to reach.

It would be easy for a seaplane to feel like a lousy boat. I know it's a silly thought since the plane was never intended to be a boat, but it occurs to me that many of us live out a logic just as silly when we settle for a life less than the one God intended us to live.

The world can throw a lot of water at us, and in the deluge of untruth, it's easy to convince ourselves we're lousy boats when, in reality, God made us something else entirely. Like the two canoes strapped to the bottom of my seaplane, I've discovered two waterproof truths to keep us afloat. First, our current surroundings don't dictate our worth, and second, we don't have to stay in a place we don't belong.

When we get clear on the value God sees in us, it changes how we see ourselves. It's like finding wings in a life you thought was meant only for water.

God loves us, but too many of us don't love ourselves because of things that have happened to us or because of where we find ourselves afloat. The good news is that we don't have to stay in those waters.

I think you're going to love the brilliant perspective of this book. My friend Bryan and I have spent a lot of time discussing the mystery of what makes us valuable. Bryan has a way of making you laugh, think, and sometimes cry, all to discover what God wants you to know about yourself. This book will entertain you, but more importantly, it will enrich you.

These chapters will change how you see value in yourself and help you understand ways God has equipped you that you probably haven't realized.

The one note Bryan continually plays in this piece of music is something we all need to put on repeat. Bryan reminds us we are priceless because of our worth in Jesus. Most of us haven't seen anything close to that kind of value in ourselves yet, which is why a book like this is important.

God loves us in any state, but since we're a lot like seaplanes, understanding the value God has placed inside will help us get to places in life that we might have considered totally off the grid.

I'm proud to be part of Bryan's debut because I think we will see a lot more of his words in the world, and those words are the kind that lift us out of the deep waters and up into the heights. In aviation terms, the pages that follow are a flaps-up, full-throttle, buckle-your-seatbelt discovery of all the value God has given you. You are in for a fun flight.

BOB GOFF
New York Times bestselling author

CONTENTS

INTRODUCTION

We Aren't Missing Any Parts

Years ago, an Italian man named Ferruccio had a successful agriculture equipment business. Ferruccio's expertise mainly involved designing tractors, but he knew he could use his skills to develop a high-powered performance luxury car.

At the time, Ferrari was the absolute standard, a well-known name in the industry. Still, Ferruccio approached Enzo Ferrari anyway and suggested ways Ferrari could improve the performance of his world-renowned car. Ferruccio believed the clutch on the Ferrari was too small for the powerful vehicle. Clutches kept burning out, and Ferruccio saw this as a design flaw. Enzo Ferrari—insulted anyone would suggest his beloved cars had a design problem—did not respond positively to Ferruccio.

Ferrari said, "You are a tractor driver, you are a farmer. You shouldn't complain driving my cars because they're the best cars in the world."[1]

Ferrari, known for his temper, exploded. "The clutch is not the problem. The problem is you don't know how to drive a Ferrari and you break the clutch."[2] Enzo was loud and animated and told Ferruccio he should stick to making tractors.

Because he knew he had the skill to design and build a high-performance car, Ferruccio wasn't discouraged. After being told he should stick to building tractors, Ferruccio manufactured the first version of his car, a 350 GTV that bore Ferruccio's last name: Lamborghini.[3]

Lamborghini was convinced Ferrari had a design problem. More specifically, he thought Ferrari's cars were missing a piece of equipment. But Ferrari didn't think his cars were missing anything. He thought Lamborghini just didn't know how to drive them. Two titans of the car industry, one with a design flaw and one with a driving problem, were both wondering about each other's wiring.

Have you ever wondered about your wiring?

There's a good chance someone reading these words has doubts about their design. Maybe it's you? Maybe you're the person who feels unequipped, who thinks life is a problem and you're inferior to solve it. Maybe you feel like cards are missing in the hand life has dealt you. The marriage hasn't worked or the career hasn't gone well, and the face you see in your mirror doesn't look happy. Less than confident, you wonder if you are missing something and ask yourself, *Is there something wrong with my design?*

There's also a chance someone reading these words has a driving problem. Maybe your engine is on, your career is going well, your family is healthy, and your bank account too. You've never had issues finding first gear, and you're someone who has felt the fast speeds of success, but you have no idea how success is supposed to carry you to the life God destined for you. Unfulfilled, you stare blankly when life asks its biggest question: "What's it all about?"

There's a good chance someone reading these words is in a

third category because you have a disconnect. You don't have driving problems, because you aren't driving. Your car is still, and the engine is cold. You haven't questioned your design, because you haven't discovered it. You live unaware, not knowing you are divinely sophisticated. Unaware of the potential heaven has handed you, you haven't yet thumbed the ignition switch to the life God intended for you to have.

Some of us don't realize we possess high-powered vehicles. A high-performance vehicle we can't drive isn't much use, and a vehicle whose design we don't understand won't take us very far. All three scenarios stem from not knowing how God wired us. Each yields the same result: a self that doesn't feel special and a life you don't love. This book is for people in all three categories because so many of us are not living the powerful life God intended.

God designed us with all the necessary components to experience lives we love. Still, most of us don't know how to operate the equipment, don't understand our capabilities, or simply don't realize what equipment we already possess.

God designed us to exist in a paradise called the Garden of Eden, where we were happy, full of purpose, and close to our Creator. We know about Eve and Adam eating the apple and understand God kicked them out of the garden. We read of God sentencing the serpent to slither on its belly, and we envision the angels guarding Eden's gates with a flaming sword, but we've missed one crucial piece. God removed humans from the garden, but he never removed anything from humans. God never reconfigured our original design. The components for experiencing happiness, harnessing purpose, and living close to our Creator are still inside us in the places he first installed them. Each feature is a piece of divinely sophisticated hardware bearing the fingerprints of the One who connected it. Over time our extraordinary parts have become buried on the inside, resulting in ordinary living on the outside. We see the results as we look over the landscape of our lives. We lack happiness and struggle to find purpose. The disconnect we feel from God shows itself in one loud voice: We don't love ourselves.

The good news is we don't need new equipment; we just need to better understand how our equipment works. We can't un-bite the apple, but we can, by God's grace, see our inner selves restored to their state when we were freshly made. A life in which we love ourselves isn't rusty and out of reach; it's just dusty and disconnected.

INTERNAL WORKINGS

A small sanctuary in Nashville called Clementine Hall has an aged apparatus that offers insight into our inner workings. When you walk through the front door, out of the bright sun, it's impossible to miss the old organ standing at the end of the aisle. The instrument filled the room as my eyes adjusted to the light, its tall brass pipes reaching high, their thickness narrowing to where they connect to a piano-like contraption.

As I looked closer, the black and white keys were familiar—I understood how each corresponded with the golden pipes standing in rows. Still, the long wooden pedals under the bench seemed out of place, and I wondered how the whole thing worked.

I've heard and seen organs played at many churches throughout my life, but standing here, I realized that how this device makes music was a complete mystery to me. I walked behind the instrument and discovered a glass panel. Looking through this window, I could see the organ's moving parts and machinery and witness how the music was made. The air forced in and out to make sound isn't visible, but it's here that the bellows breathe each note and whistle wind upward, filling first the ceiling and then the entire room with melody.

It's a beautiful scene as the wedding ceremony is about to start. The organist plays, and ushers escort guests past bare brick walls down the long white runner stretching the center aisle. They step into rows of seats arranged perfectly on oak floors and find their places. The groom stands nervously, and the bride is hidden away and waiting for her cue, but all at once, everything is interrupted. The organist is pressing keys and depressing the bellows, but the power feeding the instrument has been cut. The motor that pushes air through the pipes has stopped and the song is now silent. It's a tense moment. The sound stops even before the wedding starts, but not to worry. A circuit breaker is flipped, power returns, and air and music flow again. The organist plays beautifully, and the wedding ceremony goes off without a hitch.

As I listen to the music, I realize God constructed us like the Nashville organ. I've spent more than a decade as a hospice chaplain, and when you sit and hold someone's hand as they confront their mortality, it's like looking through a window and seeing someone's inner workings on display. Spending years at the bedside of dying people has given me a front-row view of how God designed us. I've listened to hundreds of life stories, some tragic, some triumphant, all telling because too many of us don't love our lives and don't love ourselves.

Understanding the people God created us to be is a power source for living, but this circuit breaker has been flipped for many of us. The bellows still work, and we can still press the keys, but without power, it's pointless. As a result, most of us live with a lot of effort but not much of the music we call love. All the work, construction, and design put into the organ are meant to produce music, and we are the same. All the work, construction, and design God put into us, he intended to produce love. Love is the music of the world. Love is everything. We're told that sharing this music is the highest order, told first to love God and then to love our neighbors as ourselves. For many of us, the first is easier than the second. Many of us don't love ourselves, at least not as much as God intended, and this affects how and how much we love those around us. If we aspire to love our neighbors with any success, we must first love ourselves.

Flipping the circuit breaker for the Nashville organ made for a wedding ceremony full of music. Finding the person God intended you to be will make for a life full of love for yourself. The following pages provide a way to flip the breaker and to plug in a power cord in our lives that, for many of us, has been kicked loose from the wall.

This book is an effort to share what I've seen as I've sat in the quietness of final moments and witnessed how we are wired. Our lives are spent filling our world with notes and composition for a time, but the music gets quieter near the end, and the quiet allows an understanding many miss.

I'm sharing these insights the same way I received them, through stories. People who are dying have incredible insight into how to live, and as we hear their stories, we learn how the Creator equipped us to live our own stories. I'm also sharing these stories because the people who told them asked me to. I was continually surprised to find humor woven thickly into the saddest moments. This book sometimes reads like a comedy because to truly capture how the Creator wired us is to share our saddest and lowest and our happiest and highest moments. Jesus also told a lot of stories, so I've included some of his in these chapters too.

Lamborghini and Ferrari weren't talking about our inner

workings, but their conversation could have easily been about us. Like the Ferraris and Lamborghinis, we don't have a design issue, and like the Nashville organ, we aren't missing any parts. There's simply a disconnect between who we are now and who we were initially designed to be.

If you've doubted your design, felt unfulfilled, or are unaware of the divine features inside you, this book is for you. This book will help you trade in your tractor and buckle in behind the wheel of the Lamborghini God created you to be. Imagine a life where you proudly wear your price tag instead of wondering about your worth.

NEIGHBOR, LOVE YOURSELF

CHAPTER 1

Unearthing Our Inner Worth

When I learned about a real-life treasure buried in the ground, my first instinct was to pack a bag and go looking for it. A chest filled with 265 gold coins, hundreds of gold nuggets (two of them as big as a chicken egg), Chinese jade carvings, an emerald ring, and a bag of gold dust was closed and hidden away somewhere in the Rocky Mountains north of Santa Fe, New Mexico. Hidden by a man named Forrest Fenn, this collection of valuables, worth an estimated $2 million, birthed a modern-day treasure hunt.[1]

Perhaps more interesting than the story of the treasure is the story of the man who hid it. Diagnosed with cancer and not expected to live, Forrest Fenn neared what he thought would be the end of his life and decided to leave behind something for people to find. Incredibly, Fenn survived cancer.

Alive, Forrest chose to leave the treasure where he buried it, and up until June 2020 it was still up for grabs.[2]

Fenn published a poem in his autobiography with nine clues that led to the treasure. I've never buried a treasure, but I guess after you've dug the hole, placed the riches, and left the clues, you do what Fenn did. You wait for people to find it. Fenn waited, but he did something else that caught my attention. He delighted. Fenn delighted as people came searching to find the wealth he had hidden. Every day, Fenn received calls and emails asking about the poem, the clues, and the whereabouts of the hidden chest. Fenn says one person was within 250 feet of the treasure but didn't find it. More than 350,000 people looked for the treasure; some came close, some didn't, but all searched for something they hoped would improve their lives. The reward was great, and the risk was also great—five people died while searching. Fenn, however, said his intent behind hiding the treasure was to give people hope.[3]

Hope.

The first time I heard the story of Forrest Fenn's treasure, I was intrigued by the gold and by the treasure hunt. The thought of a dying man leaving behind a treasure for people to find inspired me, but Forrest Fenn's intent to give people hope haunted me.

Hope given not just to the one who found the treasure but to all who searched for it. People were so full of hope some died searching for something they believed would improve their lives.

Fenn left clues and delighted for years in all who came to find them.

It reminds me of the treasure hunt you and I are on. At our births, God placed tremendous treasure not in the ground but inside us. Like Forrest Fenn, God does something else, something I hope will catch your attention. He delights. God delights as we search for something he has hidden inside of us that will make our lives better. Like Fenn, God offers hope not just for those who find but for everyone willing to search. Are you ready to put in effort to find the treasure in yourself? God is calling all treasure seekers, people looking for more and wondering how to find it. This is an invitation to an expedition inside yourself, one worth more than any box of buried gold. We have clues to follow and digging to do, and the first step is bringing what's been hidden out of hiding.

OUT OF HIDING

My youth group played a cutting-edge game at church lock-ins called hide-and-seek. There were three rules. Rule one, no lights allowed; this meant some areas were very dark. Rule two, stay hidden until you're found. Rule three, the last person found is deemed the ultimate hider and is given legendary status in the youth group forever. In my youth group, guys wanted to be the last found, and girls wanted to date the last found, and they would have dated them, but they could never find them.

Our God-given components can be hard to find at first because we approach finding them the same way we play hide-and-seek. We're searching, but we've left the lights off. If we want to find the valuable features that bring wealth to our lives, we must start by finding our talents. Getting clarity about the things you are good at is the equivalent of flipping the light switch. Find the things you excel at and do more of them. In the search for the features God has equipped us with, lights are allowed. Identify lightbulbs in your life by first making a list of your natural abilities. Starting an all-out expedition to search inside yourself can be daunting, but the launch of such an endeavor typically begins with something as simple as making a list.

My youth group came up with a creative name for the person searching for everyone during hide-and-seek. Some people call this person the seeker, but we were trendsetters, so we called this person . . . *It*. The game started with kids scattering everywhere, looking for places to hide as soon as It began counting to five hundred.

One kid achieved legendary status that night at the lock-in by being an expert hider. When the hide-and-seek game started, John seemed to become part vapor and vanished like a dissipating fog.

It reached five hundred in his count and shouted, "Ready or not, here I come!"

Everyone froze.

Silence.

Darkness.

It was so quiet I remember trying to make my breathing slow and shallow, so afraid It might hear me.

No sound at all until finally, I could hear footsteps.

It was in the sanctuary, and he walked to where I was hiding.

If he dropped to one knee and looked under the pew, I would face the ultimate shame of being found first.

Then salvation came as someone across the sanctuary knocked a hymnal onto the floor. The echo boomed through the auditorium, followed by muffled laughter. The seeker's feet moved quickly away from me and headed for the giggling hiders.

One by one, people were found—everyone except John.

In no way am I suggesting this is safe or recommending it should be tried today. I'm merely explaining that John achieved legendary status from which I'm sure he has drawn years of self-worth and a more prosperous life of personal glory.

He was still hiding.

We searched for *three* hours. Eventually, everyone was searching. John was hiding so long the chaperones started to worry. One chaperone walked through the church, speaking to the air and telling John the game was over and to come out.

John would go down in history as a hide-and-seek legend that night as the entire youth group and every chaperone collectively gave up and sat down on the front pew all together in the dark. Every person searched for him, and we had no idea where he was. As we sat on the front pew, the big sanctuary became silent. We had looked everywhere and discussed every possibility. We were stumped, so we sat in the quiet, big, dark church until finally one sound broke the silence—the sound of a single drop of water.

Water dripped in the baptistery on the stage behind the pulpit. Everyone jumped to their feet, rushing with realization, climbing onto the stage, looking over the baptistery wall, down into the water.

It was pitch black.

We all stood there, silence again settling over us as we peered into the dark space until It said, "Hand me that broom." It commandeered a broom leaning against the wall and began to poke at the water with the handle.

First, nothing, and then, as if a great sleeping crocodile had awoken, a thrashing sweep of water as John cried out, "Ah, you found me!"

John had submerged himself in the baptistery and breathed through a straw. He had waited underwater for more than four hours. When the lights came on, we saw John shivering; his fingers were prunes, and his clothes looked like they would never stop dripping. As John stepped out of the dark baptistery, we realized he had done something extraordinary. John had earned legendary status as the ultimate hider.

Legendary status as a hide-and-seek player is funny, but the truth is you and I already have legendary status; we were made legendary. There's a sleeping crocodile, a legend, waiting to be awakened just below the surface of ourselves, and we can wake it.

Have you ever felt the disconnect between who you are and who you could be? Those feelings are the legend inside you growing restless in its hiding place. Our true selves have been underwater and need more air than the little straw we've been breathing through can provide. To remain hidden is to be content with a less fulfilled life, one in which we never realize our full potential, one that makes it hard to love ourselves. Follow the breaths of fresh air in your life—the things you are good at, the things God has wired you with talent to do. God has equipped you with talent in certain areas, created you with skills and natural abilities. It's time to seek them out and wake your legend.

THE ARTIST WITHIN

Patricia couldn't lift her coffee cup; her hands were hurting worse than they were on my last visit. She let the cup sit on its saucer instead of risking the embarrassment of spilling, but I knew she would rather be drinking it while we talked. Even in her final days, she was dignified. I'd been visiting for several weeks and witnessed her increased discomfort. The only thing growing faster than the cancer inside her bones was the uneasiness in her spirit. Patricia told me she had been a painter in her early days when the brush was steady and she could still stand in front of the easel. As she showed me painting after painting, I found a little understanding of the many hours, the many brushstrokes, and the countless canvases she had covered with paint.

"I got a little better with each painting," Patricia said.

"Was this one of your first?" I asked.

I was holding a portrait of a young girl, one arm larger than it should be, the left ear hanging even with the chin.

"No, that's what she looked like—her poor parents," Patricia said, shaking her head.

It took me a minute to realize she was kidding. She kept her humor to the end too.

"How did you become a painter?" I asked.

"One day, I put paint on a canvas, and when I did, I felt a connection," Patricia said.

"That's how it started for you, just putting paint on a canvas?" I asked.

"That's how it starts for all of us," Patricia said.

The days passed, and cancer grew until she put down her paintbrush for the last time. Many of Patricia's paintings were hung in her room, so they surrounded her in her final hours. As I surveyed her work, I realized why Patricia painted. Her paintings made you feel something. The choice of colors and the technique of texture captured a feeling. It was as if Patricia selected one of your memories and held it up to the light so you could relive the moment. The paintings were a testimony to the skill Patricia possessed. Her pieces were beautiful, photograph-like renderings of people and scenes, all portrayed perfectly on canvas.

The paintings were wonderful, but the true masterpiece wasn't hanging on the wall or balanced on an easel. The masterpiece to behold was Patricia's discovery of her talent. The sparkle in her eyes as she spoke of painting rivaled any picture in the Louvre or any portrait by Da Vinci or Michelangelo.

I'm not a painter, but I learned some brushstrokes from Patricia. The brushstrokes Patricia showed me were not color on canvas but rather truth about living, and I think she would want me to share them with you. God placed a painter inside Patricia long before she was aware it was there. At first, Patricia wasn't a great painter; it was a talent she had to uncover over time. Like an archaeologist patiently removing the dust from an ancient treasure found in the ground, Patricia unearthed the painter inside herself one brushstroke at a time. As Patricia found this talent, she discovered other values God had placed inside her. She found her identity and confidence, and these helped her as her body began to fail and her story came to an end. She couldn't paint anymore because her hand was pinched in pain to the point she was no longer steady enough to complete a landscape, but Patricia was still a painter. The talent Patricia uncovered inside herself is still with us. Great paintings outlast the painter because the talent God has given us transcends the bodies holding them. Patricia's paintings hang everywhere. You can find them in her children's homes, on display in one of the banks in town, and in the homes of a few people who were privileged enough to watch her create them.

God delights as we discover our talents because he knows they are the first clue in a great treasure hunt. God delighted as the shepherd boy David discovered the king inside himself. He delighted as Peter, Andrew, James, and John left their fishing boats and discovered the spiritual leaders buried within. Today God delights as we discover the great things buried inside ourselves. How did David find the king inside? How did Peter, Andrew, James, and John find the spiritual leaders inside? In the same way Patricia found the painter inside herself by putting paint on the canvas. If you haven't uncovered your talent yet, start by putting paint on the canvas. Find the things you are good at and do more of them.

Like John down in the baptistery, many of our best components are hidden in places we wouldn't think to look. Are you willing to put in effort to find the treasure in yourself? If so, you may discover a talent that lives longer than you do. Let's probe with the end of our broom handles. The legendary lives God intended have been hidden from us long enough, and they need only a slight nudge to wake them. It's time to turn on the lights of our talent so we can bring the life God intended out of hiding. Go ahead, put paint on the canvas. As you do, I'm convinced you will wake your legend.

CHAPTER REFLECTION

We all have talents hidden deep inside us. But God does not intend for us to keep our talents buried. It is time to start uncovering the talents God has hidden inside you for your good and the good of the world.

1. Make a list of the areas in your life in which you have natural ability. If you have trouble thinking of areas, ask your spouse or a close friend.
2. How can you put "paint on the canvas"? What are activities, interests, or skills you are passionate about?
3. How could you engage these things for your own good and for the good of your neighbors?

Remember, having talent doesn't automatically make you an expert. Identify a starting step, an action you can take toward doing more of what you are good at, and take that step.

CHAPTER 2

Recognizing Divine Sophistication

My first lesson about the value of simple tools happened in college. One of my suitemates had a hornet nest outside his bedroom window, and the dorm we lived in wasn't air-conditioned, so we had two choices when it was hot. One, we could leave the window closed and sleep in safety, though it now felt like an oven. This choice was not great since even if you could fall asleep, you would wake up drenched in sweat.

Two, we could open the window and let in the breeze and a few hornets. The second option meant sleeping with one eye open because hornets are not like bees. If you leave bees alone, they will leave you alone; hornets don't live by that motto. Hornets sting for little reason and can sting more than once, unlike bees.

Choosing between sleeping in sweat or danger was not fun, so something had to be done about the hornets.

A college is a place of higher learning, and I found myself surrounded by prodigious thinkers. By far the wisest of my colleagues, Paul decided that if we took a vacuum cleaner and placed the hose at the end of the hornet nest, we could suck up all the hornets and then simply throw away the vacuum bag.

He said he had seen it successfully done with bees in a cartoon, and the genius of the idea was that if it had worked with bees, it would surely work for hornets. In college, cartoon logic makes sense, so we decided to implement Paul's plan. Finding a vacuum cleaner in a guys' dorm is like looking for the Loch Ness Monster. People have seen it, and you're pretty sure it's around, but good luck finding it.

We went room to room searching and finally found the oldest vacuum cleaner ever. From its look, this vacuum was used by Moses as a baby and had been somehow handed down over the generations to our dorm room. It had more electrical tape than power cord and more duct tape than hose, but it powered on when we plugged it in.

Paul's plan could have worked, as I reflect on it now. At least, it would have had a better chance of working if we had remembered to put a bag in the vacuum cleaner.

I plugged the vacuum into the outlet and slid open the window. My roommate stretched the vacuum's silver hose and inserted the end of the nozzle into the end of the hornet nest. In the first few seconds, the sound of tiny pings in the hose told us the plan was working, but our elation was short-lived. With no bag in the vacuum, the hornets were sucked into the vacuum, then were blown straight out the exhaust. In moments, the room was full of hornets.

There were so many hornets you could hear their buzzing over the sound of the vacuum; only these were no longer hornets.

We now had a room full of sucked-up and stirred-up displaced hornets who were very upset. We ran out of the room and slammed the door. Leaning against the wall in the hallway, we slid down till we were sitting on our heels and paused to catch our breath. We each had two or three stings but considered ourselves lucky, given the number of hornets we had just escaped.

We were safe in the hall with the door closed, but we still had a huge problem. The bedroom was full of hundreds of hornets who wanted to murder us.

We couldn't ignore them and had to do something, so we decided the only choice was to go to battle.

We suited up.

We put on everything we owned—sweatshirts, winter coats, and gloves.

We duct-taped our pant legs onto our socks and our sleeves into our gloves.

We put thick plastic bags (the ones my new bedspread had been packaged in) over our heads. We wrapped big belts around all the layers we were wearing, and we armed ourselves with rolled-up newspapers and flyswatters.

We looked like giant sumo wrestlers as we stepped to the door. We paused and said a silent prayer; we may have even said the Pledge of Allegiance. With our faces set and our eyebrows lowered, we gave each other a single nod and entered the room.

The hornets were angry that day, my friends.

We broke into the room with a battle cry, beating the air wildly. Flyswatters broke quickly, but not before harming hornets and leaving many dead in horseshoe patterns on the wall. The rolled-up newspaper was soon frayed, a floppy mess, and it came down to gloved hand-to-stinger combat.

Eventually the battle ended.

No hornets were left alive, and we proved simple tools could be effective. We also proved cartoon logic could work, because we found the vacuum cleaner bag and the dead hornets were sucked up and disposed of with the trash as we had initially intended.

God has placed great value at our fingertips by giving us the ability to use simple tools to do big things in our lives. Many of us never plug in the simple tools available because we don't recognize their power. God's approach looks like some kind of cartoon logic that contradicts the expectation of our human minds.

God is famous for turning a shepherd boy into a giant killer whose weapon of choice was stones and a sling.

He's known for feeding thousands of people with fish and bread borrowed from a boy's lunch.

He knocked down Jericho's walls by telling his people to walk around them thirteen times, and he healed blindness by rubbing spit in people's eyes.

At first glance, God's plan to save humanity looks like cartoon logic. How else do you explain God sending the Savior to be born in a barn and sleep in a feed trough?

What we call cartoon logic is God revealing his sophistication in simple tools.

Watch Jesus work.

He doesn't need a crash cart, adrenaline, or CPR to bring someone back to life. He doesn't need an operating room or X-rays to make people walk again. The tools Jesus uses for these things are simple phrases like "Come out," "Get up," or, in the case of the wild storm on the Sea of Galilee, "Be still."

Accomplishing big things using simple tools can look like cartoon logic, but the most straightforward tools—a whisper, smooth stones, a manger, or a few fish—have divine sophistication when God places them in our hands.

Moses learned this lesson directly from God. "The LORD said to him, 'What is that in your hand?'"[1] Moses was holding a simple tool, a walking stick, a tool he used a lot. God showed

Moses how to turn his walking stick into a snake so Moses could demonstrate God's power to Pharaoh. Moses used his stick again to turn the Nile into blood because Pharaoh needed more convincing. Moses used the stick to part the Red Sea so the Israelites could escape slavery and, later, to bring water out of a rock so the Israelites wouldn't die of thirst in the desert. We often feel under-equipped in our lives, but we can't discount the great things God can do through the simplest tools at our fingertips. If all you have is a flyswatter, an old vacuum cleaner, or a walking stick, in God's eyes you're well equipped. The challenge is recognizing the tools we have in our hands. A few years ago, a dying man showed me a tool all of us have the power to use in our lives.

ONE SIMPLE TOOL

Richard was the head of a company whose name you'd recognize. Richard had expensive cars in the driveway of a house many would envy, and servants surrounded him. Each time I visited Richard, his groundskeeper offered to park my car, his executive assistant met me at the door, and his house manager asked if I wanted something to drink. Richard traveled around the world on his private plane, owned houses on multiple continents, and vacationed in countless countries. The paintings on the walls cost more than anything in my checking account, and the bathroom on the ground floor of Richard's house was likely worth more than my entire house.

As I entered Richard's room, I knew this would be the last day of his life. If brokering deals and draining bank accounts could give any leverage as his lungs bargained for one more breath, Richard's family would have gladly paid it, but deep pockets couldn't change the fact that Richard's breathing was shallow and all the money he invested couldn't earn one more heartbeat.

Richard's wife hugged me, her eyes swollen, her mouth smiling.

"He's been waiting for you," she said.

Over the past three months, Richard and I had been having a conversation. There were pauses as I would leave and return a day or two later, but it was the same discussion. Richard was telling me his life story, and I was listening. Today we had reached the end of the story.

"What has been the secret to your success?" I had asked days prior.

"It comes down to how successful you are with what you have on hand at any given time," Richard said.

There were those words again. The message God had spoken to Moses, Richard was saying it to me now.

Richard used the phrase "Using what you have on hand," which was almost verbatim to God asking Moses, "What is that in your hand?"[2]

Sitting in the big house, I had to know. What was the tool Richard held in his hands to produce such a successful career?

"What did you have on hand?" I asked. I expected Richard to tell me about a nest egg of money that helped him get started. I assumed Richard would say something about a market that was right for his product or maybe an investment tip that paid off big. Richard cleared his throat and found enough breath in his failing lungs to speak.

I leaned in.

"The same thing we all have on hand—time," Richard said.

Another breath and then another sentence.

"I put time into my marriage, I put time into my children, and I put time into my business," Richard said.

When a man running out of time tells you time is the most

important tool, you remember his words. Richard's advice offered me a dividend more valuable than dollars. We all have time on our hands and would do well to give this valuable tool to our marriages, ministries, children, and churches. We feel under-equipped because our tools seem simple, yet we give away moments and minutes, perhaps our greatest investable assets, to things and places that will never help our families or ourselves.

Have you recognized what God has placed in your hand?

For Richard, it was time.

For me, it was a flyswatter and an old vacuum cleaner.

For Moses, it was a stick.

For the boy hearing Jesus speak, it was his lunch.

For the world, it was a baby in a stable, destined for a cross.

God designed us with the ability to do amazing things with simple tools. We can create complex organizations, lasting relationships, and dynamic, healthy families, and we can do all of these with what we have in our hands. The irony is most of us haven't recognized the tools we have even though we are holding them.

What is in your hand? What is your walking stick? What's one simple tool you could be using in your life?

I learned an investment tip from Richard, and I think he'd want me to share it with you. Simple things let God's complexity shine. We wait for God to give us more; God waits for us to realize the value in what we already have. Does your life feel like it's lacking value?

We often feel God is asking us to be satisfied with less, but God is telling us we already have more than we realize. We've convinced ourselves that some of our skills have passed their prime, like the old vacuum cleaner we searched for in my dorm, but this isn't true. God can use whatever we have in our hands, old, big, or small, no matter the color or condition of our talents.

God is standing with us in the hallway, and he's waiting for us to realize the value we have in our hands, waiting for us to step into a room where we can be used.

There are a lot of doorways as we wait with God in the hallway.

God's waiting for some of us to step into the room with our youth groups.

He's waiting for some of us to step into the room with our communities.

He's waiting for some of us to step into the room with our families.

He's given us everything we need for what's waiting on the other side of the door, and he wants us to open the door and step into the room. God doesn't expect us to show up with a master plan; he just wants us to show up. We don't need high-tech tools; simple ones like time and love will do. Using simple tools can sometimes seem like something out of a cartoon, but don't let that stop you.

If you are unsure where to start, take Richard's advice and start with time. As you do, I believe you will recognize a great value in using simple tools to accomplish big things in your life.

CHAPTER REFLECTION

Have you ever felt under-equipped? It's easy to feel like the deck is stacked against us, the odds are not in our favor, and our journeys are always uphill. Feeling this way over time can lead to two things: a discouraging feeling of pending defeat and a lack of confidence that results in feeling like we are less.

1. What tools do you have at your disposal? What do you possess, which might seem lacking in value, that God might use for your good or the good of others?
2. Consider an area in your life where you have been waiting on God. Is it possible God is waiting on you to use one of the tools he's already given you?
3. How has God moved in surprising ways in the past? How might he do so in the future?

God places great power not high on a shelf but at our fingertips, where it can be used. God's examples show us there is nothing he cannot use. As you take inventory of the tools God has given you, ask him to help you use them for his glory and the good of the world.

CHAPTER 3

Good Words

When the Lovett family built their house in Livingston Parish, Louisiana, they wrote seventy scriptures in permanent marker on the bare wood two-by-four framing in the walls. In February 2020 the house caught fire and burned for five hours, but the flames stopped when they reached the wooden studs.

When this story aired on the news, I'm sure many dismissed it as coincidence, happenstance, or even fraud, but the surprise the firefighters found told a different story.[1] As the men from the Livingston Parish Fire Protection District shone their flashlights through the smoke and water-drenched debris, they were overcome by what they saw.

"What caught our eyes was that the homeowners had written scriptures on the wall studs throughout the house. The fire stopped at the scriptures!" a representative from the fire department said.[2]

Firefighters who brought hoses and water and worked for hours battling the flames were surprised the fire stopped when it reached the words inscribed on the two-by-fours.

God isn't the only one writing on our framework. Some of us have written words inside ourselves that aren't true, words God would never write. We've written words like *failure, hopeless,* and *lost cause,* and in some cases, we've written them in bold print and underlined them. In the worst cases, some of us have gouged them into the wood so deeply that we now believe these fictions to be fact. We've listed our mistakes in detail and built our entire houses around them. The result is houses made of cards where God intended fortresses no fire could burn. When the fires of life threaten us, we doubt the confidence of our construction. We must embrace the fire-stopping framework our Father first made in us. Our inner words are meant to protect us from external fire.

What words are written on your two-by-fours? Like the house in Louisiana, we have inner frameworks, and many words have been written on the beams of our beings over our lifetimes of construction. When we peel back the drywall, wave away the dust, and shine a flashlight on the wooden beams of our frameworks, we find something profound.

God designed our internal frameworks with two purposes:

- First, to fireproof our identities.
- Second, to motivate us to move us forward.

If you've felt burned or feel like you aren't moving forward, it's likely time to double-check the words written on your inner framework.

Time for a home inspection, perhaps one that will lead to re-modeling. Open your desk drawer and take out a trusty yellow number two pencil. This yellow dinosaur, this ancient artifact, was perhaps once used to fill out the bubbles of standardized tests like the SAT and ACT. It may seem low tech, but your pencil has two essential functions—writing and erasing. In the context of your framework, it's time to erase internal fiction and rewrite eternal truth. Here are a few words to get you started: *intelligent, talented, trustworthy, strong, honest, good,* and *beautiful.* You'll likely find that some of these words have already been written inside you and just need to be underlined or bolded. You'll also find a lot of blank spaces in your framework, places where God encourages us to do some writing. What will you write in these areas? Teacher, doctor, drummer, and dancer are great inscriptions, and there's plenty of room to write these things. Write whatever you want as long as you write truth. Look for the load-bearing beams of your internal construction and write more powerful words like loyal, loving, and selfless. Don't forget the pink eraser on the end of your pencil as you survey your internal structure. Look for opportunities to flip your pencil around and erase untruths. With our erasers, we can rub out the lies written on the boards of our inner frameworks. As we write truth and erase fiction, we will add strength and momentum to help us move forward.

God intended our core identities to be fireproof. Knowing there will be times we feel the flames of life and are burned almost to the ground, God created internal identities that no fire can torch. Like firefighters' protective gear, specific words that God has engraved deeply into our frameworks can help us withstand the fires in our lives. His fireproof truth includes words like *loved, valuable,* and *extraordinary* that have been etched deeply into our inner beings. As we wear these words, they shield our inner identities as fires spring up around us. Cloaked in their protection, we can run forward, untouched by flames that would otherwise consume us. If you are facing fire and can't move forward, take a second look at the words God has written on your framework.

GOOD WORDS MOVE US FORWARD

When you become a big brother or sister, a line is added to your résumé: "In charge of introducing siblings to new things." You get the job, but no one tells you how to do it.

As a big brother or sister, you fumble and find your way by taking your younger sibling, a sister in my case, wherever you go and conducting "let's see what happens" experiments.

Safety is not the top consideration, and both older and younger siblings will agree it's impressive how many younger brothers and sisters have survived this old system.

One of my "let's see what happens" experiments didn't go very well. I am not proud of this one.

My mom and dad gave me an electric slot-car set for Christmas one year. The cars ran on an oval of black plastic with two metal-lined grooves running the length of the track. If you had one when you were a kid, you probably remember that each race car had a little metal post hanging down from the bottom to connect to a groove on the track. Pushing the button on the remote control with your thumb released electricity that traveled through the groove, up the little metal post, and into the car. The electricity powered a motor that turned the small rubber wheels, taking the car around the track. It was cutting-edge tech when I was eight, and we loved it.

Around this time, my dad introduced my sister and me to the wonders of a nine-volt battery. My sister and I giggled as we touched our tongues to the battery's metal posts, feeling the current twinge, tingle, and numb our noses. Because of my experience with the nine-volt battery, I'm sure you can understand why I wanted to see what would happen if I told my sister to place her tongue in the racetrack's metal groove. If the tiny battery was fun, a racetrack plugged into the wall would be way more fun.

My sister followed my directions without question, but when I pressed the button on the remote with my thumb, she didn't giggle.

She kind of froze and got this watery-eyed stare.

I now understand her blank stare indicated electrocution.

One major flaw in big-brother experiments is they are not things you try only once. I'm sure the guidebook for the experiments tells you to repeat until laughter or tears. So I am ashamed to admit that I pressed the button again, and there were tears as my sister rode the lightning again.

My sister is brilliant, and she's alive, by the way. Like Victor Frankenstein harnessing the lightning to bring his creature to life, I like to think that I awakened parts of my sister's brain dormant in non-racetrack lickers.

Over the years, I've said, "You're welcome" to her for the race car track experiment, but she gives me a blank stare when I say it. Maybe she's having a flashback.

God designed us to run on the power of good words. One of the most powerful forces in our world is good words.

This isn't accidental. Good words are like the electricity flowing through my old race car track. The power in our good words may not be visible, but it can move us forward.

As we say good words to people, we unleash an electricity visible on their faces.

When I dropped to one knee and said, "Maggie, will you marry me?" her face lit up (thank goodness). Maggie's eyes and expression told me she would say yes before she said the word.

We know the good words that move us:

"It's a girl!"

"State champions"

"Cancer free"

"I believe in Jesus."

"You're hired."

"She said yes."

Good words make eyes twinkle, voices laugh, and cheeks blush red. We cannot see the electric power found in our words; we know it's there because we see the result of this power. When we internalize the words written inside of us, we experience inner combustion like a spark igniting gasoline in our car engines, because God designed our internal engines to run on good words and to move us forward in life. When we've become slow, stuck, or still, it's because we've gotten bogged down in the untrue words we've believed about ourselves.

With his words "Let there be light" still echoing off the newly created mountains and canyons, God surveyed all he made, and two words came to mind. The Bible says, "God saw all that he had made, and it was very good."[3] God looked at the earth, sky, animals, and humans and thought all of it was "very good." We seem to forget God's original opinion of us was a very good one. We need to stop letting other people's bad thoughts about us cover up God's "very good."

Erasing untruths and rediscovering true words God has written on our inner frameworks are good ways to tap into the power of good words in our lives. We all need to surround ourselves with people who will pour heaping helpings of good words into us so there is less room for bad words to take root. Surround yourself with people who will speak good, true words about you. Immerse yourself in good words, those spoken by others in the present and those written down by God in the past.

CALLING OUT THE GOOD WORDS

We have a bedtime ritual at our house. After Casey brushes her teeth and I tuck her under the covers, fetch a second drink of water, and sing a second song, I sit on the edge of my daughter's bed and whisper good words to her.

I lean close to the towel twisted up around her hair. I sweep my hand over her eyes so that they will close, and I whisper good words to her as she drifts off to sleep. I usually start by saying, "I want to tell you some things I love about Casey." A small pause and then more whispers. "I love how smart she is; I love how kind she is. I love how she loves her momma and how sweetly she treats little kids." I tell her I love how much she loves Jesus and what a great singer she is. Every night, as the fish tank filter whirs in the background and the night-light casts its dim glow, I spend a few minutes whispering to the small head that's finally found its pillow.

I point out all of her good traits and tell her I'm proud of her and that she's special, loved, and valuable. Those words are already there; God has already written them inside her. I'm simply reading them aloud. I've seen them written on her character, and I'm calling them out so she will recognize them. I want Casey to hear those words enough to believe they're true. I want to unleash the power of the good words inside her, a power God has given.

I've wondered if God spoke in a loud voice or quietly when he spoke the world into existence, and as I'm putting Casey to bed, I think I've figured out he spoke in a quiet voice. When I speak good words to Casey each night, I say them aloud. I'm speaking in a whisper in the dark, but good words spoken are so powerful a whisper is enough.

CHAPTER REFLECTION

Most of us have a pretty good memory when it comes to the bad words people have used to describe us. As a result, we let these untruths hold us back. Perhaps it is time to ask God to erase these words from our vocabularies and begin looking to him to reveal the value he sees and has instilled deep inside us.

1. Call out three untrue words that you have inscribed on your inner framework. How are these words holding you back from the life God has for you?
2. Name three true words God has written on the beams of your being. How might these words help you move forward into the life God has for you?
3. What is one way you could remind yourself of the good words on a regular basis?

Don't let the worst things others have said shape how you see yourself or how you live. Ask God to help you see the tremendous value he has instilled in you. Ask him to help you live like you matter to him and have much to offer the people around you, because you do.

CHAPTER 4

Bad Words

F rank was holding on, but barely.

"How much longer till he gets here?" Frank's daughter asked.

The question hung in the room unanswered as the small group gathered around Frank's bed and waited. There was nothing to do now *but* wait. Wait as Frank's heart slowed, wait as the pauses between breaths increased, and wait for whatever Frank seemed to be waiting on.

"Jimmy will be here soon," Frank's wife said, leaning close and whispering the words near the head of the bed. She kept fluffing Frank's pillows and straightening his blankets, but I doubt Frank cared about either of those in his current state.

Near the end of life, the body shuts down in stages, usually over a period of three weeks. In hospice, we call the final stage "active dying." Blood pressure drops significantly during the actively dying stage as patients slip into a semi-coma, are increasingly hard to wake, and have long pauses between breaths.[1] Frank had been in this stage longer than most. There was no medical reason for Frank to be living; fluid had built up in his lungs, and his hands and feet had become rigid, but he was still holding on.

Frank's wife and daughter came after I called with an update on Frank's condition and had been with him for two days. Other members of Frank's family had come too; they were all here, all except one. Frank's son Jimmy had not joined the vigil, and as the hours passed and Frank didn't, it became increasingly clear we were keeping vigil for Frank, but Frank was keeping his own vigil for his son. I watched and waited with Frank and his family. Later we'd learn we were waiting on Frank's son to say two words.

Solomon is famous for saying the power of life and death is found in our tongues.[2] I witnessed this truth that night at Frank's bedside. Many of us spend a lot of time waiting for words we wish would come from someone who hurt us. We allow unsaid words to hold us in place like an ancient anchor, forgetting we have the power to untie our boats and float away at any time. Jesus died to give us a new future and a new present, but most of us still let past hurts hold us hostage. I've learned that, for some people nearing the end, forgiveness is harder to believe as it gets harder to breathe. For some reason this is an easier concept to understand when our lungs are working well.

Jimmy made it to his father's room late that evening, and from the look of his eyes, he had cried the entire trip. Years of bitterness had built up brick by brick until they stood like a wall between Jimmy and his father. Neither was innocent; both Frank and Jimmy had put a lot of time into building the barrier that had separated them for years. The wall seemed massive with its many bricks of pain, regret, and hurt, but in the end, none of the bricks in the wall were strong enough to stand. The entire wall came crashing down in seconds as

Jimmy saw his father on his deathbed and said two words. Jimmy fell across his father, crying, saying over and over, "I'm sorry. I'm sorry. I'm sorry." The words came in sobs, some audible, others muffled, as Jimmy cried them into his father's chest and blankets.

Later I would reflect on how Jimmy had spoken his words with his face pointed directly to Frank's chest, directly to Frank's heart. No wall or coma could stop Jimmy's "I'm sorry" from reaching his father, and Frank passed away moments after Jimmy said the words. We watched as his body relaxed and his breathing stopped. The words Frank had been dying to hear for so many years became the words he spent his last days living to hear, and having heard them, he died in peace. Frank couldn't say any words in reply to his son, but the final moments of his life spoke volumes. He had hung on. He had kept breathing and kept waiting for his son to arrive.

Solomon was right. Our words do have the power to bring life or death. Good words can keep us living, and bad words can hurt us so deeply we fight to erase them before moving on. Too many of us have let our lives become slow, stuck, or still from bad words. We've felt the freeze bad words bring. The numb feeling after the girlfriend says, "I'm breaking up with you," the heart-pounding silence after the doctor says, "We've found a spot on your lung," the stinging words delivered by the husband who says, "I don't love you anymore." Bad words hurt and stop us in our tracks.

Bad words were never part of our original design, and they don't belong in our inner workings. We've given them too much authority, too much weight, too much hold. As seen with Frank and Jimmy, bad words will weigh heavily on us for years if we let them. The takeaway from this truth is clear. If we ever hope to break free from the bonds of bad words, we have to surround ourselves with an abundance of good words. If we don't, one or two bad words will hold back our entire stories. I learned this with the first book I wrote.

TWO BAD WORDS

The book you are reading is not the first I've written. I wrote a funny children's book you can find on Amazon. The book is a bedtime story illustrated by a talented artist named Jessica Flannery. It's a story I used to tell my daughter, Casey, at bedtime. She is proud of it because she helped create it.

When Casey was in third grade, she wanted to share the book and the pictures with one of the kindergarten classes at her school. Casey asked her teacher for permission to read the book. The teacher talked it over with the principal, and they decided Casey should read the book not just to one class but to all the kindergarten classes. The plan was to gather them together in the school auditorium so Casey could read the book from the stage. There was talk of projecting the pictures on a big screen so everyone could see, and even a plan to give Casey a microphone so all the kids could hear. Casey loved the idea, and I was thrilled. Only one problem—the principal read the book. After reading it, she decided it was not appropriate for kindergartners, not just the kindergartners in her school but kindergartners everywhere. Casey's class was already aware of the book, and many of her classmates had bought it. Since other copies of the book were circulating in the school, the principal banned my book first from the kindergarten classes and then the entire school.

The first book I wrote was banned from its first audience because of two bad words.

My daughter was disappointed.

To be honest, I was a little embarrassed I had written a children's book that had been banned for language. Ironically, that principal was fired a year later for using one bad word—the f-word. The principal was recording a phone announcement and thought the recording had finished. The principal, unfortunately, could be heard using the one bad word at the end of the message. It was probably something the administration could have forgiven, but when the phone announcement went out to all the parents, everyone remembered only one word in the message, the bad one. Bad words are dangerous. They have power in our world, and they shouldn't be used or given power over our lives. They can cripple an entire message or story, and that is something we cannot allow as we live out the stories of our lives.

What were the two bad words in my first book?

The book is called *Stripey Bottom.*

Here is a sample for your consideration:

"Doctor, Doctor! Come quick. Something's wrong!" said the nurse.

The doctor rushed down the hall and into the room.

"Let's have a look," said the doctor.

The nurse lowered the baby's diaper. "What is it, Doctor?" said the nurse.

The doctor frowned. "I'm afraid . . . it's a bad case of . . . Stripey bottom."

"Oh no! Is there anything that can be done?" said the nurse.

"I need you to go to my desk. Look in the top right-hand drawer. I need you to bring what you find there to me," said the doctor.

"What am I looking for, Doctor?" said the nurse.

"Quickly! We don't have much time!" said the doctor.

The nurse ran as fast as she could down the hallway. When she returned, she was out of breath.

"Here you go, Doctor," she said.

The doctor took the item from the nurse's hand.

"Do you think this will work?" said the nurse.

"Let's hope so," said the doctor.

The doctor took the eraser from the nurse's hand. He began erasing the stripes from the baby's bottom.

"It's working! It's working!" said the nurse.

"We're not out of the woods yet," said the doctor.

The doctor kept erasing, and then suddenly, the nurse let out a shriek.

"Oh no! Doctor, look!"

"Yes, I'm afraid I've erased too much. This baby's butt crack is gone."

The story goes on from there . . .

I'm biased, but I've shared *Stripey Bottom* with many children, and they've all responded with laughter. Still, two words prevented us from being able to share this laughter with an entire school. I think that's the way it is in our lives.

We tell our stories with hundreds and thousands of words, but many of us have let one or two bad words stand in the way of our entire stories. Words like "not smart enough" or "not talented enough." It's funny how so many of those statements end with the word *enough*. If you take out the two bad words, the word *enough* is all that remains. We're enough. Good enough. Strong enough. Smart enough. Our Creator made us this way, but we have to remove the bad words that come before *enough* because they're standing in the way of our stories.

Those bad words were never accurate, and believing them as truth is not what God wants for our lives. Have you let a couple of bad words hold back your story? The bad words may be spoken or unspoken. Maybe you've said them to others; perhaps you've said them to yourself.

The way Frank died taught me something about living, something I think he would want me to share with you.

The wall between Frank and Jimmy took two people to build. If we're honest, we can all point to walls to which we've added bricks made of bad words. We all have walls we've built or are building, barriers that stand in the way of moving forward. Like Jimmy and Frank, we've built walls between our relationships but also walls inside ourselves that prevent us from seeing our potential. Our "I'm not" statements make great bricks perfect for building barriers. We all build these barriers for different reasons, but they don't belong in our lives. When God made us, he didn't include any "I'm not's"; we added those later, so we need to tear down any wall built with these statements.

At Frank's bedside, I witnessed a wall, one that kept Frank from dying, but I think we've all had times we let walls keep us from living. Taking down walls can seem like hard work, but Jimmy and Frank would tell you it takes removing only a brick or two to topple an entire wall.

Don't wait till your deathbed to take down the walls that don't belong.

Like every good story, our stories have good and bad parts, action, drama, and hopefully a little comedy too. The world around you needs to hear your story, and who better to tell it than the author? Don't let one or two bad words stand in the way.

CHAPTER REFLECTION

Have you let a couple of bad words hold back your story? We all have at some point. Call them out into the light. If the bad words were spoken about you, find someone you trust and ask if there is truth in those bad words. You will either discover the bad words are lies or you will identify something about yourself you can change. Either way, you will take away the power the bad words have held over you.

1. What are examples of bad words you've let stick in your mind or influence your view of yourself?
2. What could you do to limit the influence of these bad words? What good words could you replace these bad words with?
3. Have you built up walls against other people with the bricks of bad words? How so?

Perhaps walls separate you from someone you shouldn't be separated from. There is still time to remove the bricks. The best method for bad-word brick removal is to surround yourself with good words. Use them when talking about yourself, and use them often. Next, use them in big heaping piles to describe and build up the person you have had bad blood with. Doing this over time will help bring down the walls that have separated you.

CHAPTER 5

Purpose Power

When you stand in a typhoon on roller skates holding a garbage bag over your head, you're not sure where you'll end up, but you know it will be a great ride.

Wind power was a big part of my childhood growing up in Okinawa, Japan. During typhoon season, surging storms with names like "Charlie" or "Doris" brought roaring rain and category-four-strength wind plowing inland. In category four, typhoon winds were too dangerous to brave, but days prior, at category two, the strong wind was nothing but fun. With winds strong and only beginning to gust, I'd tell my sister to grab her roller skates and a big trash bag from under the kitchen sink. "Is it safe?" she asked.

"Come on; we're missing it," I'd say.

As the lightning flashed, I'm sure she had reservations; this was the same person I had once asked to lick the electric race-track. I guess once you've tasted electricity, you think twice about tempting lightning.

With arms extended, we would stand at the end of our street on our skates and hold our trash bags in the air. The wind filling the bags and snapping them into a sail was as loud as a starter pistol as we were propelled forward by the typhoon. Gripping white-knuckle tight to the trash bags, we were in for a fast ride if we could stay on our feet.

Finding purpose is like harnessing a typhoon. God designed us with a sail to harness the winds of purpose and drive us forward, farther, and faster. When we find purpose, work is rewarding and dedication is endless. The energy you need for your job, the enthusiasm you crave for your ministry, and the excitement you want for your life are all winds God wired us to harness. If you feel stuck or unable to move forward, don't take off your skates. The winds of purpose are all around, but we need to determine the direction of those winds if we hope to capture their power. This chapter is a wind sock intended to help you find the direction of your purpose and move forward.

GRAVE SYMBOL

Nestled in the English countryside of Worcestershire lies a grave that offers insight into finding purpose. The headstone near the Church of St. Michael stands out—it's the only grave marker with drumsticks instead of flowers. It's the grave of John Bonham, the drummer for Led Zeppelin. He died in 1980. Fans pay tribute by placing drumsticks and cymbals atop Bonham's headstone every year. Looking at Bonham's grave, I find symbolism in the cymbals. I wonder what people would leave on my headstone. Whether you're a Zeppelin fan or not, there's little denying John found something he loved to do and devoted his time and energy to it. Judging by record sales and the tokens left at John's resting place, people admired him for making this life choice and sticking to it. If you're having trouble finding your purpose, ask yourself what you want people to leave at your grave. What do you want to be known for? What do you want people to say about you after you're gone? Start at your grave and work backward to where you are now.

The things we love to do are often the winds of purpose God has set our sails for. List five things you love to do and determine how much time and energy you're putting into those things. If you want to move forward in life, consider doing more of the things on your list.

Pastor and author Myles Munroe once said,

> The wealthiest place on earth is the cemetery. It holds the treasures that people never served to humanity.
>
> It is wealthy because buried in the cemetery are books that were never written. In the graveyard is music that no one had a chance to hear, songs that were never sung! The graveyard is filled with magazines that were never published. The cemetery is filled with businesses that were never opened. What a tragedy![1]

Munroe is right. Within our cemeteries, poems that could have motivated lie unfinished, movies that could have inspired sit unmade, and life-changing ideas and inventions rest incomplete. People won't leave copies of your book on your gravestone if you never pick up your pen. No one will stand at your grave and sing your song if you never write it, and no playbills will be left on your headstone if you never audition for the part. Too many of us don't love our lives because we are in the process of taking our purpose to our graves. Doing less of what we love leads to a life rich with regret, and it's a shame when we place our talents in coffins instead of sharing them with the world. Flowers are lovely, but I want something instead of flowers at my gravesite. Not drumsticks and cymbals, in my case, but something that represents what I loved, what I was passionate about, something that represents my purpose. It's not about decorating my final resting place. It's about ornaments that testify to a life spent doing what God designed me to do.

I met a woman, as she was nearing the grave, who had advice on this subject; her name was Mary. She lived near Front Street in Marietta, Ohio, and when I met her, she still had a lot of life left in her mind but not her body. Mary was a nurse.

"I'm not retired," Mary said.

"You're still working?" I asked, not understanding.

"I don't get paid to do it anymore, but I'll always be a nurse," Mary said.

"What do you like most about being a nurse?" I asked.

"Like it?" asked Mary.

"Yeah, what are your favorite parts of the job?" I asked.

Then Mary found energy.

"For me, it wasn't a job; it was who I was, so it wasn't about liking it or not liking it," Mary said.

"You mean you liked it even on the bad days?" I asked.

"No, you hated the bad days and loved the good days, but all of it was the same package for me."

Mary told me stories from her twenty-five years as an ER nurse, each one gorier and more tense than the last. Mary told the stories with a combination of pride and compassion. Compassion because she had an inner desire to care for hurting people and pride as she told of the skill she used to help them. Mary went to nursing school and learned how to care for people. She developed her skill with every experience and every patient who passed through the emergency room doors. The more people Mary helped, the more her expertise grew and the more Mary was equipped to help. I went to Mary's funeral. She had joked about having the words "I'm still a nurse" carved on her tombstone. She may not have had the words en-

graved in granite to mark her grave, but she had spent twenty-
five years etching the words into her life. Mary had discovered
a truth I think she would want me to share with you. Mary
called herself a nurse, but for her, identity was more than her
occupation. Mary proudly wore the title of nurse because it fit
her chosen identity of caring for others. Many people at Mary's
calling hours smiled as they passed her casket. They smiled
because Mary was wearing her stethoscope.

John Bonham is often quoted as saying, "I remember in the
early days when we played six nights a week for a month and I
was doing my long drum solo every night. My hands were covered in blisters."

Finding purpose is about finding something you don't mind
getting blisters doing, the trade whose tool you'd happily be
buried with. So how do we find our drumsticks and stethoscopes?

We may think finding our purpose happens through divine
revelation with bright lights as we journey on the road to Da-
mascus, but that's often not the case. No sorting hat like in
Harry Potter telling you what house you're supposed to be a
part of. No high council of elves, dwarves, and wizards meets
to determine if you're meant to carry the ring to Mordor as for
Frodo, and there's usually no Obi-Wan Kenobi who hands you
your dad's lightsaber and tells you about your destiny.

We assume finding our purpose is like that, but it's simpler,
as simple as picking something you connect with. It's finding
what you're good at and doing more of it; it's realizing what
you love and saying no to the things you don't. As we create
more moments centered on these things, we add up days and
months of purpose. I guess I'm saying that finding purpose is
a choice many of us never make because we're waiting for
Frodo's ring, Luke's lightsaber, or the Hogwarts sorting hat,

and none of those things can tell us what's truly important to us or what we love.

Mary got into nursing because she cared about people. Knowledge and skill came later. Mary's story ended with a stethoscope she couldn't put down and a title she'd never give up, but it started by simply finding something she cared about and sticking with it.

God doesn't provide an on switch, but he does provide on-ramps. God designed us with free will so we can choose the things we want to dedicate our time to. Pick an on-ramp and commit to riding that road. Mary was a nurse even on the bad days, and John was a drummer even when he got blisters. When it comes to purpose, it's typically not bad days or blisters that hold us back; it's wind blockers. Wind blockers are the things standing in the way of our purpose. We all deal with two common wind blockers at some point in our lives, and I want to call them out here so we can step in front of them and hold our sails high.

TWO WIND BLOCKERS

Two things keep us from catching the wind of purpose in our sails.

FEAR

We're afraid of failing, afraid of not being given a chance to succeed, and afraid our talent will go unrecognized. We're afraid to try and afraid to fail. We're afraid of being afraid. It's natural to be afraid, but God never intended for our fear to prevent us from finding our purpose. God did not intend us to live in fear, and he tells us repeatedly not to fear.[2]

"Don't panic. I'm with you. There's no need to fear, for I'm your God. I'll give you strength. I'll help you. I'll hold you steady, keep a firm grip on you."[3]

When you are fearful, remember that God keeps a firm grip on us as we get a grip on our purpose. Trust the One who tells us not to be afraid, pick an on-ramp, pick up a drumstick, and go for it.

DOUBT

The second wind blocker is doubt.

We'll talk more about doubt in an upcoming chapter, but doubt will stand between our sails and the winds of purpose if we let it. We all doubt. We doubt ourselves, our choices, and our futures, and faith is the only voice that can speak louder than doubt.

"But when you ask, you must believe and not doubt, because the one who doubts is like a wave of the sea, blown and tossed by the wind."[4]

Don't let the waves catch the wind meant for your sails. If you're still having trouble making your list of five things you love to do, here are other areas where you can look to help you find clues to your purpose.

NATURE ALLOWS US TO FIND OUR PURPOSE

Nature isn't a purpose, but it can help us find it. Since humankind originated with a clear and distinct purpose in a garden, we still have echoes of our connection to creation deep in our DNA. We notice it at an elemental level when we reconnect with the earth.

Whenever I sink my feet deep in the sand at the ocean's edge or hike a secluded trail in the mountains, I feel my peace power up. For me, such hikes are soothing and waves wash tension out to sea. It's in these peaceful times that I can reflect on my purpose. Finding the things that bring peace to your life can point you toward purpose.

You probably have specific places in God's creation where you feel a stress release too. Nature alone doesn't hold all the answers, but it's the perfect prescription as we search for some of them. We're part of God's creation and constructed to connect with it.

Have you ever asked someone how their vacation was and heard them reply with a one-word answer, "Peaceful"? Usually, the one-word answer is accompanied by a dreamy look in their eyes as if they're trying to teleport back to their vacation spot mentally. Most people who give that kind of answer have been somewhere in nature. They've disconnected from the distractions and found an environment that allows for reconfirming purpose.

PEOPLE WE TRUST POINT US TO PURPOSE

If you're still unsure, ask people you trust what they think your talents are. Listen closely to what people say you are good at, and when different friends point to the same traits, tune your time to that station. Ask your parents what things you initially gravitated toward when you were a child. We outgrow some strengths, and some we have our entire lives, so knowing your backstory may be helpful. What have you received thank-yous for in your life? We typically receive thank-yous when we've met a need for someone, so thank-yous often point to found purpose. Maybe you were a counselor who gave great advice or excelled in listening.

God created us to love good things and do good work, and God smiles as we identify the things we love and work at them.

Push back fear, throw off doubt, and capture the wind. Start the business, write the book, sign up for the audition, take the guitar lessons, teach a class or take a class, or quit the job. Don't neglect to care for the people who depend on you, but as much as you're able, find good, positive things that make you feel fulfilled, and do more of those. The winds of purpose are blowing all around us, and we can harness their typhoon-type power to move us forward. Hold your sail high, point your skates toward the horizon, and hold on white-knuckle tight because it's sure to be a great ride as you harness the power of purpose.

CHAPTER REFLECTION

Take a moment to stop and consider the things you most love to do. How much time and energy are you putting into them? While you surely have obligations you must attend to that keep you from doing these things all the time, it is likely you could be more intentional with your time. It's time to start dreaming about how you might give more time to the things you love for the glory of God and the good of the world.

1. What do you want people to leave on your gravestone? Why?
2. What are the drumsticks and stethoscopes in your life, the tools of the trade you were born to do? How might you create more margin to engage in something you love?
3. Have you encountered the wind blockers of fear and doubt? When was the last time you gave those fears and doubts to God?

Get out in nature. Talk with people you trust. Identify the things you are good at and the things that bring you peace. These are weather vanes pointing you in the direction of purpose.

CHAPTER 6

The Power to Picture Our Future

Ruth's daughters are here as the doctor steps out from behind the blue curtain hanging around Ruth's bed. He's pulling the curtain open, and tiny metal hooks make a *scritching* sound as they slide on the track in the ceiling.

Fear frames the faces of this family as the doctor speaks to Ruth's daughters.

"She's resting now," the doctor says.

"How much time do we have?" one of Ruth's daughters asks.

I'm not sure either daughter hears the answer; they don't need to hear it, because they can tell these are final moments with Mom.

Ruth's eyes are closed, her mouth is open, and her breathing is shallow, short, and labored. The lungs and heart that have done their work for more than ninety years are tiring. We listen to lengthening spaces between Ruth's breaths, waiting and watching for her chest's next rise and fall.

Sounds interrupt the silence.

The door *whooshes* closed as the doctor leaves.

Sniffles accompany the onset of tears.

Ruth's daughter asks me to pray with them.

I pray and the sniffles grow louder. By the end of my prayer, everyone is crying.

Ruth's daughter is holding her mom's hand and mine, and I can feel her shaking as she cries harder.

I end the prayer with an amen, and all at once, Ruth says, "Amen" too.

Ruth's eyes are open, and she's mouthing words I can't understand.

"What is it, Mom? We're right here," Ruth's daughter says.

We are all leaning in as Ruth clears her throat, her voice shaky as she says, "I see all of you, but one of you is bright."

"What do you mean, Mom?" Ruth's daughter says.

Ruth continues, "I see you, Rachel, and Emma, and him."

"This is Bryan, Mom; he's here to pray with you," Rachel says.

"I see him too, but one of you is bright," says Ruth, her voice clearer now. Now she's holding out her hand, not to Rachel or me or Emma but up.

"Is she dreaming?" Emma asks.

"He's right beside you, Rachel," Ruth says. Rachel looks over her shoulder and then at me with a questioning gaze. Rachel doesn't see anyone, but it's clear Ruth does.

Ruth is puzzled; she doesn't understand why Rachel isn't seeing what she's seeing.

I watch Ruth's hand. Her ninety-year-old hand, tired, wrinkled, spotted with age. It's the hand Rachel and Emma know well. This hand stroked Rachel's and Emma's hair when they were sick, patted their backs to quiet them when they were babies; this hand taught them to sew and bake. This is the hand they held a lot when they were young and have held again in recent days as Ruth neared the end.

Ruth's hand is reaching for someone.

Her fingers and thumb close slightly, and it looks like she's holding someone's hand, or rather it looks like someone is holding her hand.

Then Ruth breaks the silence in the room with an incredible and out-of-place sound not heard for some time. Ruth giggles. Her daughter's cheeks are still wet with tears, and Ruth is giggling. The sound coming from Ruth is not a laugh from a ninety-year-old, but it's the sound of a child skipping rope or dancing in a field of flowers or splashing in a pool on a summer day. This is the sound of a baby playing peekaboo or a toddler playing tag on a playground. It's the sound of carefree joy. Ruth's giggle is so sweet and rich; it has turned the tears in the room into smiles. Tears or not, Rachel's eyes couldn't open any wider as she stares at her mom. Emma's hand is frozen at her chest, holding a crumpled tissue that has no new tears to wipe away.

Can there be laughter in the face of death? Ruth would tell us there can be. We've assumed all our life stories will end in tears, but maybe we've assumed this because we don't understand our future in front of the curtain.

There were two curtains in Ruth's hospital room that day—the blue paperlike curtain hanging around the bed and a second curtain, one not as easy to see but just as present and perhaps as thin.

The second curtain was the one separating the world we see and the world we don't. Angels do their work behind the second curtain. It's the second curtain hiding a realm our human eyes cannot detect, and someone pulled back the second curtain on that day as we sat by Ruth's bed. Emma, Rachel, and I couldn't tell the curtain had opened; there was no *scritching* sound as the curtain was pulled back, no breeze or bright light. We didn't know the second curtain was open, but Ruth did.

Someone, an angel or maybe Jesus, stretched a hand out from behind the curtain and extended it to Ruth.

Seeing Ruth by the second curtain has given me a new perspective, one I think Ruth would want me to share with you. We don't have to wait to see what our lives will be like at the end of our stories. We can visualize the end of our stories now. Imagining your ending may not be appealing, and perhaps it seems a bit depressing, but it's because we haven't understood what's waiting behind the second curtain. There is a greeting coming. A welcoming. I don't know if it's a single angel or a group of holy hosts or Jesus himself who lifts the curtain and welcomes us home, but I do know an escort from heaven will meet you at the threshold of the curtain.

Does that surprise you? If you have wondered about your worth, think for a moment about the welcome that is waiting. For dignitaries, we roll out a red carpet. We put on parades, raise the curtain, and spotlight center stage to help our most honored guests feel welcome. If we do this on earth, how much more extravagant is the welcome for one for whom the Prince of heaven was crucified? It's a celebration, a moment Jesus died for, and it's all in your honor. The moment when a lamb who was lost is brought back into the fold. The final part of God's master plan is welcoming you home, and judging by the expression on Ruth's face, the welcome rekindles childlike laughter. Laughter that dissolves years of age, pain and sadness, wrinkles and worry. Laughter that testifies to the pure joy you will have upon your first glimpse behind the curtain.

Can you see it? Can you visualize the end of your story? You may be in a hospital bed like Ruth. You may be in your bed at home. Some of our stories will end while cutting the grass or driving to the grocery store. Some will end at work, church, or any number of places and scenarios we've composed in our life stories. No matter the place, the experience is coming for all of us. The thin curtain will part, and a hand will reach out from the unseen world and into this world.

God has given us our imaginations to picture ourselves at the edge of the curtain, to gain perspective on the end of our stories. You gain motivation when you sit beside the thin curtain separating this life and the next. If you don't like the future picture, change your present.

Ruth let go of Rachel's hand and took hold of the hand of the one who was "bright."

If not an angel, maybe it was Jesus. He's preparing a place for us. We know he'll return officially one day; the Bible is clear on that. But what's to stop Jesus from kneeling and peeking behind the curtain occasionally?

I don't know if it was an angel or Jesus, but one of them was there for the end of Ruth's story. As Rachel, Emma, and I sat at the bedside, Ruth was allowed to walk behind the curtain. We watched Ruth's final words, watched as her laughter changed. It aged. No longer a giggle but the chuckle of an elderly lady. Not a full laugh but half of one. There was discovery in this laugh. Something between a grin and an "aha." I heard relief in Ruth's laughter like a sigh of contentment. Like settling into your favorite chair after a long walk on sore feet. Ruth smiled, settled into her bed, closed her eyes, and let her hand sink to her side. She slept and soon passed. Ruth's body remained with Rachel and Emma, but Ruth was no longer on this side of the curtain. Ruth walked hand in hand with the One who is bright.

What does the end of your story look like as you picture yourself beside the curtain? Who are the people gathered around your bed? Are you laughing? Are you ready to walk with the One who is bright? If not, change the ending of your story. We can live differently now to make a better ending later.

STEPHEN AND THE SPARTAN RACE

My friends and I were in the starting blocks with fifteen minutes to spare. In moments the starter pistol would fire and we would run five miles, the first half of it up the side of a mountain, through thirty obstacles, a riverbed, and several mud pits.

"Are you nervous?" I asked Matt.

"We got this," Matt said back.

I noticed he didn't answer my question and decided it was better not to know if he was nervous. Knowing he was uneasy would only make me more uneasy. I didn't need to know anyway; we were nervous.

We were antsy, stretching and laughing when my friend Stephen decided it would be funny if he had a picture taken of himself crawling on his belly across the starting line.

"It'll be hilarious—it will look like I'm dragging myself across the finish line after a brutal race," Stephen said.

Everyone agreed it would be funny.

"Just wait, and you won't have to fake that picture; it will be your reality soon," said Matt. We all laughed as he said it, but a few of us wondered if we would end up with similar pictures capturing our reality.

It was a fun idea, and the picture is even funnier now because when Stephen crawled across the starting line, the electronic sensor he was wearing on his arm, the one designed to time his race, beeped. The sensor had activated, signaling the start of Stephen's race.

When the race official holding the starter pistol heard Stephen's chip activate, he pointed toward the racecourse and up the face of the mountain and yelled, "Your race just started; you gotta go!"

The runners in the starting blocks watched and pointed as

Stephen started the race alone. All eyes watched as he began to run the first mile straight up the side of the mountain. As people realized Stephen's race had started, everyone began to root for him. "You got this." "Go, Stephen!" "Save us a seat at the finish line!"

Though he didn't know it, Stephen illustrated a truth about life and how we value ourselves. God has destined us for great things, but many of us have not started yet. We struggle to see the talent inside ourselves because our deepest dreams lie dormant. We aren't completing the work we were made to do on the outside because we haven't realized on the inside that we are capable of this work. Disconnected from our dreams, we are unknowingly living at half capacity.

If you struggle to believe in yourself, your capabilities, or your worth, maybe picturing the finish line will help you crawl across the starting line. A publisher is waiting to publish the book you need to write. A company is waiting to mail the offer letter for the dream job you need to apply for. Wedding invitations are waiting to be sent out, announcing your big day, but you need to ask the person on a date first. Imagining yourself completing these things can be a first step across the starting line. God gives us the ability to picture our futures so we know what we are running after. What are the things you want to complete by the time you reach the curtain? Paul said to throw off anything standing in our way, especially if it is sin related.

Therefore, since we are surrounded by such a great cloud of witnesses, let us throw off everything that hinders and the sin that so easily entangles. And let us run with perseverance the race marked out for us, fixing our eyes on Jesus, the pioneer and perfecter of faith. For the joy set before him he endured the cross, scorning its shame, and sat down at the right hand of the throne of God. Consider him who endured such opposition from sinners so that you will not grow weary and lose heart.[1]

The starter pistol is raised, and you are standing in the blocks. Your race has begun. You have a cloud of witnesses cheering you on, and the One who is bright waits to welcome you at the finish line. Run.

CHAPTER REFLECTION

What are things you'd like to accomplish in life that you fear you never will? Have you ever considered you might be selling yourself short? Maybe it is time to make a list of the things you want to accomplish and imagine yourself completing them.

1. What are the things you want to complete by the time you reach the curtain? Make a list and prioritize what's most important.
2. Are there any barriers standing in the way of the starting line? How can you throw these off?
3. What are the biggest time wasters in your life? What is one step you could take this week to be more intentional with your time?

God has given you the ability to picture your future so that you might know what you are running after. When you imagine your future, what do you see? Take a moment to pray, asking God to give you a vision for where you want to go and what you want to accomplish this week, this month, this year.

CHAPTER 7

The Power to Paint Our Present

If you've ever felt like you're losing your mind, remember it's the masterpieces painted by insane artists that we value the most. Keep painting.

Vincent wasn't allowed to paint in his room, but he couldn't stop thinking about the brightness of the morning star he had seen from his window before sunrise. Vincent, moved by the sight of the star, wrote to his brother Theo about it, "This morning I saw the countryside from my window a long time before sunrise, with nothing but the morning star, which looked very big."[1]

Inspired, Vincent started painting the star from memory, applying paint directly to the canvas from the paint tubes. In the observation room of the insane asylum, Vincent stepped back from the easel and looked at his creation. The curvy cypress tree in the foreground, the glowing star, the crescent moon, the rolling countryside, and the swirling sky all surround a tiny town. The image Van Gogh captured on the canvas has captivated people for almost a hundred years. *The Starry Night* is arguably the most recognized painting in the world and has taken on a life of its own, now displayed on T-shirts, coffee mugs, screen savers, and just about everywhere you can think of. It's fitting *The Starry Night* is everywhere you can imagine because the painting came from Vincent van Gogh's imagination. The tiny town in the painting doesn't exist, or at least it didn't until Vincent brought it and the image of the morning star out of his memory and into reality.

Van Gogh used a paintbrush to bring a world he imagined to life, and we can do the same today. God equipped us with a paintbrush we can use to bring the lives we imagine for ourselves into reality.

Interrupting the silence of nothingness with his voice, God painted the masterpiece of creation. No construction crews with concrete or builders with blueprints, wearing holy hard hats. Gazing at the blank canvas of darkness, God, with his voice as his paintbrush, brought the universe's brilliance into existence. Before God said the word *light,* there was no light and no term for it. He invented light by speaking its name. God spoke aloud when he created the world in the universe, even though no one was around to hear him speak. In the ultimate demonstration of their power, God used spoken words to make our world.

Since God created us in his image, we can also create with our spoken words. If you have ever wondered about your ability to create, know that a paintbrush comes standard as part of our design. We can't exactly go out and create Jupiter or Mars by speaking their names, but we can create with our words. We may not invent new elements or universes, but we can paint into existence the lives we have imagined for ourselves. We have dictionaries for countless colors, hues, and shades to paint with, so our words offer an endless array of options for creating our masterpieces.

If this sounds a bit crazy to you, don't worry, this is not a mystical séance or incantation, or some hocus-pocus, heebie-jeebie kind of voodoo. Far from it. I'm talking about a God-given ability to shape our lives with our voices and words. If you don't love your life, perhaps you haven't discovered your painting abilities yet.

To his disciples, Jesus explained the power of speaking to our problems: "If anyone says to this mountain, 'Go, throw yourself into the sea,' and does not doubt in their heart but believes that what they say will happen, it will be done for them."[2] We have the ability to speak to the world around us. Speaking aloud what we believe focuses the power of our faith like a magnifying glass focusing the sun's rays. There is a time for silent prayers, but speaking aloud gathers our faith and delivers it with pinpoint accuracy.

As we face mountain-sized problems, Jesus tells us we can use our spoken faith to move them. We know the mountains we need to move. Mountains like sickness, relationship problems, finances, and addiction. They don't belong in our paths, so let's send them to the sea. Remember how David spoke to his mountain? His peak was named Goliath, a giant who looked undefeatable. David said, "This day the LORD will deliver you into my hands, and I'll strike you down and cut off your head."[3] David's words leave little doubt about how he felt about the mountains standing in his way. Many of us ask God to remove the summits in our way, but we haven't spoken directly to the mountains ourselves.

TURN THE LIGHTS ON

As I look at Van Gogh's *Starry Night,* I see something else that applies to us as master painters. In the tiny town beneath the starry night, all the lights are on except the lights in the church.

In Van Gogh's imagination, the church was dark.

I don't know what problems your church is facing (though I could venture a decent guess), but I know you and I possess the power to turn the lights on. I'm not talking about turning the physical lights on. I'm talking about the places and the people around us we can, and should, illuminate with our words. We can bring light, and it's a good thing, too, because critical areas need it.

Some of us need to turn on lights in the minds of our students with bright words of encouragement. Others should enlighten the souls of their children with beaming acts of love, and still others must switch on lights in the hearts of their spouses with brilliant displays of affection.

I don't know why the lights are out in the tiny *Starry Night* town church, but I do know there are churches in each of our towns that look similar. The churches in our towns were meant to shine bright because, as master artists, we can make them shine. Debate can be good, but when minor points of doctrine or religion become louder than the voice of Jesus in our lives, it's time to be quiet. Arguments over doctrine and denomination can dim our churches, and disagreement about religion can make us dark. Jesus is light, so if we want to bring light back to our churches, we must put aside anything that overshadows him. Maybe this is one of the mountains you were meant to move. If so, speak to your mountain with the voice God has given you. God's first words were about light. Since Jesus is light, let our first words be about Jesus. Speak Jesus to the people in your church. Not religion, not doctrine or denomination, just Jesus.

GIVE LIKE YOU HAVE NOTHING

Gertie could make coffee without a coffee maker or hot water.

"Fujas in ya cup," she would say as she handed me a glass. Since it wasn't hot, Gertie could serve coffee in a regular glass. She was saying "Folgers in your cup," the famous tagline from the coffee commercial, but the combination of not having any teeth and her Appalachian accent made "Folgers" sound like "Fujas."

I'd been to Gertie's house enough to form a ritual. I'd sit at the kitchen table, a card table, in one of two lawn chairs, and Gertie would grab the small jar of instant coffee from the windowsill. After twisting off the red cap, Gertie would scoop out two spoonfuls of powder, one for her glass and one for mine. It wasn't Folgers, just an off brand Gertie would pour out of a bag into the Folgers jar.

With glass in hand, the real work of drinking it began. It was nearly impossible to stomach, and I dreaded the drink the entire thirty minutes it took to drive to her house. The instant coffee crystals never dissolved into the cold tap water, and the floaters would stick and strain between your teeth with each sip. The trick was to drink just enough. Drinking too little would insult my host, and I figured the measurement of being respectful was to drink the concoction to about half a glass.

Gertie's father was dying, and her small income was taken quickly by the things he needed. I think that's why the wealth I found in Gertie's words was so profound.

One day, as my glass was half empty, I asked her, "Gertie, what makes you so generous?"

"None a' what I have is mine anyhow," she said. "That man in the livin' room taught me dat." She pointed her finger to where her father was sleeping.

Hanging in her kitchen over the sink was a handwritten sign that read, "I have all I need, and God has the rest."

"I like your artwork," I said, pointing to the sign.

"Thank you," said Gertie.

"I got all I need. A roof o'er my head and a bed for my dad," she said.

I meant what I said. I liked her artwork, but it was a statement about more than the handwritten sign over her sink. Gertie was a painter, and she had covered her canvas with color and light.

I couldn't help but think of the story Jesus told of the widow who gave her last penny. Jesus told the story to his disciples so they would understand the widow had given more than the rich because she had given the very last of what she had, and in Jesus' eyes this made her a hero. I wondered if the widow in the Bible was like Gertie.

"You remind me of one of the heroes in the Bible," I said.

"Thoot, I ain't no 'ero," Gertie said. I was sure she was trying to say *shoot* instead of *thoot* and *hero* instead of *'ero.*

"All we got is borrowed; I just learnt it sooner than most," Gertie said.

"You mean the things we own?" I asked.

"We don't own anything," Gertie said.

I thought she was talking about herself at first, but I realized she meant me too.

"The bank owns your house till you almost dead, and you sure don't own it when you buried, so we just borrowin' it," Gertie said.

"I guess that's true for our bodies too," I said.

"You got dat right, and when we done with it ain't nobody wants that either." When Gertie said this, she laughed a wheezy, full-bellied laugh that made me smile.

She didn't think so, but Gertie seemed heroic to me. Gertie

wasn't depressed about her situation or angry about her life. As I sat at her kitchen card table, she told me jokes, we laughed, and I saw the light in her eyes and joy on her face.

Gertie's father passed away and I saw her only a few times after the funeral, but I think of her often. Like the coffee crystals stuck in my teeth long after our conversations, something about Gertie stuck with me. Gertie had nothing. Her possessions consisted of two lawn chairs, a card table, a few changes of clothes, instant coffee, and one more thing. Gertie had something all of us search for and many of us miss. Gertie was content.

Maybe that's hard for you to believe, but though Gertie's canvas was sparser than most, she had covered it well. She could shape her world in a way finances or circumstances could not touch because, for Gertie, finances and circumstances did not determine her contentment. She made a home out of nothing, shared love and warmth, and had no regret. If Van Gogh were to paint Gertie's little trailer in a scene, the lights inside would be brilliant and blinding.

I think Jesus asks us to give him everything so we can discover a truth Gertie understood. When we give Jesus everything, we love ourselves more, and contentment comes easier when our possessions and circumstances are not our primary concerns. Gertie had nothing, and that included no regrets. Too many of us regret things we own, we don't own, situations we are in, situations we wish we were in, and scenarios we wish had never happened. Too many of us are down on ourselves because of what we earn or don't earn, and the result is lives we don't love.

A SECOND COAT

My first name isn't Vincent, and I'm certainly no Van Gogh, but I paint. Oh, I'm not an artist; I don't paint on canvas but rather on the walls of my house. I may not be considered a master artist, but I've painted enough rooms over the years to know a thing or two about paint. When I want to paint an entire room, I go to the hardware store and select a color from the thousands of samples. The clerk always asks if I want primer too. Without primer the old color bleeds through and makes the job harder.

In our life's painting, belief is the primer. The more belief we have in our words, the more effective they are at transforming the canvas. Load up your words with lots of bright colors of belief. Become part painter and part prophet, declaring to yourself the picture of what's coming next. When we load our paintbrushes with words and belief, the makeover begins and the lights in the town of our masterpiece glow. I've seen some good painters in my time. Good painters stand out because we see great paintings in their lives.

It's the friend who battled cancer and beat it.

The mother who dug deep in prayer and now celebrates her son's return from his life of drugs.

The wife smiling as she stands next to the baptistery as her husband, who was once a nonbeliever, stands up, soaking wet after baptism.

Nothing is stopping you from becoming a masterful painter. Finances are no match for the primer of belief, and circumstances cannot darken the light of Jesus. Select colors you'd like to see more of in yourself. Speak those words into your life, maybe into your mirror, and definitely into your prayers. Remember, we do the painting but it's God who transforms the canvas. Take out your paintbrush and speak good words into your world. Inform yourself and others of what you're creating. As you do this, God will create the reality you crave. As you believe the words you are saying about yourself, you will see a transformation; you're going to unveil your masterpiece.

CHAPTER REFLECTION

What are the areas that need light in your life? Remember that a wall takes two or three coats to paint. Without primer the old paint bleeds through and the room resists transformation. Belief is our primer. Speak positive words into your life repeatedly; there's nothing wrong with repetition until the belief comes.

1. How often are you speaking the light of Jesus into the dark places in your life?
2. How much do you believe the words you are saying? What is one step you could take this week to deepen your faith?
3. What steps could you take to foster belief and a deeper trust in God's guidance and provision?

Remember that in your life's painting, belief is the primer. The more belief you have in your words, the more effective they are at transforming the canvas. Ask God to load up your words with lots of bright colors of belief.

CHAPTER 8

The Power of Failure

I was on the John Muir Trail in Yosemite Valley again, trying for a second time to reach the top of Half Dome. I told myself this time would not be like the last. I'd put in the work, spent months conditioning and eating healthy, and even bought better shoes. I was right about one thing. This time did not turn out like the last.

In 2015 my wife and I made our first attempt to hike Half Dome but were disappointed. We started too late in the day, and sunset forced us to turn around before reaching the top.

I couldn't escape Half Dome. Whenever I turned on my laptop, a picture of the half-round rock reached out to me. The company The North Face takes its name from the north-facing wall of Half Dome; its logo (the silhouette of Half Dome) greeted me every time I wore my winter coat, and I was wearing my coat a lot. Half Dome haunted me.

Have you ever had a goal that haunted you? A dream or desire you promised yourself you would reach? Maybe for you it's getting a college degree, landing a job promotion, losing weight, getting out of debt, or running a marathon. Giant granite-faced goals are worth chasing; after all, God gives us the abilities and talents to accomplish such things. Goals are good, great even, but we are in dangerous territory when not reaching them affects how we see value in ourselves. My Half Dome experience helped me discover this concept.

My hiking group hit the trail hours before daylight shone on our shoes.

My pack was light when we reached the mist of Vernal Fall.

My legs were strong hours later as I climbed the steps past Nevada Fall, and my energy was steady for miles into the wilderness as we reached one mile in elevation. I was no less determined as we reached the last section of the hike—a rugged rock staircase of switchbacks and steep stone steps. The base of Half Dome, with its sheer rock face and cables leading to the top, was next, but I never made it that far.

As I looked at the steps, each about three feet wide, I realized there was only enough room to hike single file, or so I thought. I soon found myself turning sideways to share one of the small steps with a descending hiker. Facing the sheer drop-off, I felt the full exposure of the elevation. Going up, I could focus on my feet and not the long drop below, but when I shared the three-foot step, for the first time I looked over my shoulder to the drop below, and froze.

I visualized myself slipping off the step and falling almost one mile to the rocky valley floor below. I imagined a long, horrible fall, full of time and terror the whole way down. I didn't just imagine it, though; I felt it. I felt the fall approaching, felt the fall becoming my reality as my legs grew weak and started to shake.

Paralyzed, I crouched down, wanting to secure myself to the safer stone of the step.

I could hear my heart beating, feel the pulse as loud as an alarm, and realized I couldn't overcome my fear of falling long enough to climb back down. One mile up in the open air, on top of a mountain with nothing but the blue sky in every direction, and I felt claustrophobic.

Frozen, I couldn't climb or descend, so I slid my back down the cliff wall and sat on my heels.

Have you been there? Have you ever had your boasts silenced by the freeze of fear? We all do, and when we do, we find ourselves sitting on our heels, halted by our inadequacies. Your New Year's resolution of getting in shape is hamstrung by a pulled hamstring on your first run. Your plan to move ahead at work is put in park by the person HR says is "more qualified." Your dream of a prestigious education is canceled when the acceptance letter never arrives because your grades weren't good enough.

We are good goal chasers, but in our exuberance to excel, we've forgotten about the power of failure. As adults, we are not skilled at using failure, but we didn't begin life this way. As toddlers, we learned to walk by failing, not by perfecting crawling. We don't trash-talk babies who fall and fail as they learn to walk, but we trash-talk ourselves as we fall and fail. Failing exposes areas where learning is needed, but for some reason, we unlearn this as we age. The truth is God designed us with the capacity to learn and grow from our failures. Some of our best minds have figured this out.

Gandhi described failure as a blessing from God. Thomas Edison viewed failure as part of the process of finding the right solution, and Einstein is often quoted as saying that failure is "success in progress." These brilliant minds discovered that God intended failure as a blessing, as part of the process of succeeding and learning. Failure isn't the lack of success; it's learning.

Most of us don't define failure as learning. This change we've made over time in the definition of failure shifts the focus from the free environment of learning to an ultimatum of success.

Think about the last time you failed. Was it a failure, or was it a loss of learning? If failure has crushed your ego or bruised your pride, I suspect you, like me, have some redefining to do. This seemingly small change will shift failure from an ego buster to a talent builder. We need to reset our definition of failure to its original meaning—the one God intended. Neglecting to do so comes at a cost. The cost is a loss of love for God's most prized creation, ourselves.

While we have changed our definition of failure, God has not. God isn't disappointed when we don't reach the elevation or status we've set for ourselves. God doesn't see us this way, and it's not how he wants us to see ourselves. We need a new perspective. We need a new lens.

THE LEARNING LENS

When you sit in the optometrist's chair, the doctor swings a machine out from the wall that looks like giant owl eyes; it's called a phoropter. The phoropter has lenses to help us see up close, lenses to improve our vision farther out, and different lenses that flip back and forth to help us determine the level of correction our vision needs.

God programmed us with a phoropter so we can view our lives through different lenses.

If we touch the glowing red rings on the top of our kitchen stoves, they burn and hurt. We have a magnifying lens in our phoropter, one best for looking at fresh blisters. A magnified view helps in treating our burns so they can heal properly. Still, while the magnifying lens is suitable for understanding our mistakes and applying ointment to our injuries, we must switch back to a different lens after examining the results of our failures.

If we continue to view our situations through a magnifying lens, we have a distorted view of ourselves. A magnified view shows the burns, blisters, and scars in a full frame. Since we are much more than our scars, the magnifying lens we use to assess our failures isn't the right one for moving forward. If we move forward with a magnified view, we will always see our mistakes as bigger than they are and, in doing so, will destine ourselves to live under the delusion that we are now less after having failed when, in fact, we are more because of it.

What is a failure? Are you a failure if you don't make it as far or as high on the mountain as you intended? Are you a failure if you are slower or faster, taller or shorter, richer or poorer than the people around you?

No. I'm convinced God intended failure as feedback we can use to move forward. We will fail at things no matter how hard we try or prepare. With each failure comes a lesson to better prepare us for the next mountain.

BORN OF FIRE

The morning after I failed to reach the top of Half Dome, I woke up and went through the motions. Breakfast with friends, coffee, and then a drive to Mariposa Grove.

At Mariposa, God flipped the lens in my phoropter so I could see failure as he intended. We'd spent the day before hiking for thirteen hours with cramping quad and calf muscles. Now we walked only a few minutes on soft, flat dirt till we stood at the base of one of the largest trees on the planet. Grizzly Giant is a massive sequoia standing 209 feet tall with a trunk 30 feet in circumference. Three thousand years old, it was alive when Jesus walked the earth. Grizzly Giant dominates Mariposa Grove with its bulging biceps-like branches hanging with moss and age. Walking toward the trunk, I marveled at the size of this tree.

Fresh from my failure, I wondered what a tree that had lived three thousand years had endured.

Pictures and plaques surround this tree. Pictures of Teddy Roosevelt standing where I planted my feet now and plaques telling of the tree's origin and history.

One plaque explained that giant sequoias grow out of a seed the size of a pinhead and grow only if triggered by fire and planted in the ashes of the burned seedpod. Without fire, the seed will not sprout; without the ashes, it won't grow to become a giant sequoia.

Another plaque next to Grizzly Giant is dedicated to Mariposa Grove's firefighters. For years, firefighters worked putting out fires in Mariposa Grove until they discovered that the more fires they put out, the fewer giant sequoia trees were growing. Without fire, the seeds never sprouted. What would be the ultimate failure for other seeds is an essential requirement for the birth of a giant sequoia.

God designed the giant sequoia to respond to fire in the same way he created us to respond to failure.

Without failure, we can't reach our Grizzly Giant–sized potential. We see failure as a fire burning us to the ground, a setback eliminating our path to success, but that perspective is the wrong lens.

Watching my friends pass me at the base of Half Dome, I felt the burn of failure. I kept hearing this inner voice telling me I wasn't tough or brave enough to make it to the top. The magnifying lens distorted my view. Without switching from the magnifying lens, all I could see was an up close view of the last part of the hike, the part I didn't complete.

We don't see failure the way God does. Humankind kicked out of paradise is a failure, and if we look only through the magnifying lens, we'll miss the Grizzly Giant God has grown out of the ashes of Eden. At first glance, Jesus dying on a cross seemed like a failure, too, but when we look through the far-seeing lens, the one God uses, we find a much bigger plan that God envisioned long before Jesus walked the earth. It appeared that Jesus' ministry burned to the ground and died with him on the cross. His body was planted in the ground along with his followers' faith, but from the ashes of the tomb, Christianity sprouted. A seed of hope pushed out of the soil through the opening in the earth the rolled-away stone created. A Savior who survived the tomb sees failure much differently than we do. Jesus sees our failure as fresh soil and nourishing ashes for future growth.

I took a second look through a broader lens at my Half Dome experience. As I stood in the ashes of my failure, I felt something sprout inside me. Standing in the shadow of the Grizzly Giant, I found the words I needed for a chapter in this book, but more importantly, I found words I needed for a chapter in my life.

All of us are trying to reach the top of one mountain or another. Some of us will make it on the first try, and some will climb a different mountain. Our climbs will reveal failure as future footholds. Sometimes not reaching the peak on the outside helps us get a peek at the inside.

There's a Grizzly Giant in the book you're holding. I thought hiking Half Dome would be one of the hardest things I would do. It turns out writing a book was much harder. There was a sequoia-sized dream inside of me as I sat frozen on the step, but it took the failure of Half Dome to find it.

The life God intended for us isn't one where we stop failing; it's one where we fail better. If you haven't reached the top of the mountain you are climbing, it's okay. Keep learning, keep climbing, or find another mountain. If your ashes are still warm from the fires of failure, don't give up. God has assembled all the ingredients you need, and you are likely about to see something sprout.

CHAPTER REFLECTION

For most people, failure is something they run from or avoid at all costs. God, however, intends your failures for your good. When you bring faith to your failures, instead of holding you back, your failures can instruct you, make you stronger, and help you grow into the person God created you to be. With that in mind, what are your top three biggest failures?

1. Have failures made you love yourself any less? How so?
2. How have you defined yourself by your failures in the past? How might redefining these failures change your future?
3. Would changing the definition of failure from "unsuccessful" to "learning" change how you feel about your failure? Looking back, what can you learn from these failures?

Your failures don't have to define you. They can fuel you to a better, fuller, more focused life. Instead of being held back or paralyzed by your failures, ask God to help you learn and grow from them.

CHAPTER 9

Castle of Confidence

Ohio isn't known for castles, but thirty minutes north of Cincinnati, on the banks of the Little Miami River, stands a castle built entirely by hand.

The castle is called Chateau Laroche, built by a man named Harry Andrews.[1] Harry's story ironically starts with his death, or at least it was assumed Harry was dead. Harry was a medic in World War I, and in 1918 he contracted spinal meningitis so bad it left him blind, paralyzed, and unable to speak. The U.S. Army declared Harry dead and sent him to the morgue, but the army made a critical mistake, and the proof came during Harry's autopsy. As the scalpel cut into Harry's body, he began to bleed, something the dead don't do. Nursing Harry back to health took time, but waiting on the army to inform the world Harry was still living took longer. It took so long for the news of Harry's "resurrection" to reach the United States that his fiancée married another man.

Harry left his home, country, and true love to fight in a war. The United States won, but Harry lost a lot, and the worst loss for Harry was his fiancée.

The war ended, but with no woman to return home to, Harry decided to stay in Europe for a while. Maybe it was the war crushing Harry's defenses or the pain from losing the love of his life; perhaps it was the effects the pulverizing punch of being presumed dead had on his self-esteem. Whatever the reason, something about the castles in Europe appealed to Harry. What caught Harry's attention was the ancient majesty in the time-tested walls; even modern bombs had not brought them down. As Harry spent months touring castles in France and England, he discovered an aged strength not from medieval times but biblical ones. The strength found in tall turrets, daunting drawbridges, and water-filled moats was impressive, but Harry discovered something deeper, something older, an ancient code the knights who once defended these castles lived by. At a time in his life when things were dark, the code Harry found was a light. At a time in Harry's life when outer defenses were destroyed, Harry found an inner fortress. Harry adopted the knight's code as his own and deemed it the code of the Knights of the Golden Trail. To travel the golden trail was to live with chivalry, high ideals, and a dedication to the Ten Commandments.

When Harry finally returned home, he realized it wasn't only his life that was missing the strength found in the knight's code; Harry thought the world was missing it too. An intelligent man with an IQ of 189, Harry surmised the best way to change the future was to start with the hearts and minds that would be leading it.

Who would you start with if you wanted to change the world? Where would you begin if you were going to embark on a quest to shape young hearts and minds for the future? Harry began by teaching Sunday school and leading a Boy Scout troop. He connected with his students, and together they started the Knights of the Golden Trail. KOGT invited "any man of high ideals who wishes to help save civilization" to join them.[2] By 1928 there were more than one hundred members of the Knights of the Golden Trail. They met so often that Harry eventually decided he wanted to give his knights what all knights need, a castle. "In the 1920s, *The Cincinnati Enquirer* offered plots of land along the river to anyone who paid in advance for a year subscription."[3] Harry acquired eleven of these lots and started building.

Harry and the knights hauled fifty-six thousand buckets of rocks up from the Little Miami River, carried fifty-four thousand buckets of dirt, and mixed twenty-six hundred sacks of cement. Carrying and mixing these ingredients is impressive, but there was another ingredient Harry moved and mixed more: love. Harry's love for his knights, and his love for making the world better, sustained his building until he built high tower walls and sturdy stone stairways leading to lookouts, archways, and hallways. Harry's castle included a dry moat, a keep, a meeting room, and battlements all cobbled together by hand.

The result was an impressive castle—one built out of love.

As I stood in the shadow of the walls Harry built, I realized we all want a solid stone strength in our lives. Life often takes much and leaves loss, and our first instinct is to surround ourselves with walls for protection. We want walls of self-assurance, something substantial that will sustain us. In a world where people let us down, we want to keep them out, so we build. We stack stones higher and keep people at a distance, thinking confidence will come. Stone walls can keep people out, but if we're being honest with ourselves, our work in building walls feels a bit cobbled together. I think I know why.

To find confidence in our lives, we don't need external walls; we need internal strength. We can't build externally to protect our internal selves, because our external is earthly and our internal is divine. There simply is no earthly barrier big enough to protect heavenly treasure.

After experiencing what Harry had gone through, most people would've built walls to keep others out, but Harry built walls to invite others in. He invited all to find strength, a strength not found in the mixture of mortar, the hardness of concrete, or the height of stacked stones. As I ran my hand over the rough rocks at Chateau Laroche, I realized Harry's strength was not in the stone but in the code by which he lived. The same is true for us. We wish walls were the answer, but confidence doesn't come from castle walls. Confidence comes from the code we live by. Jesus doesn't offer a code of commandments but one of forgiveness. Our Savior comes to us in our darkest times, offering an inner fortress when our outer defenses are destroyed.

Are you in need of such a code? Are you craving a confidence that can't be built externally?

It's easy to understand why we build castle walls in our lives. Heartbreak, trauma, betrayal, ridicule. These are the soldiers life assaults us with, sometimes to the point we are presumed dead. Paul certainly felt this. In one of his letters, he wrote:

We are hard pressed on every side, but not crushed; perplexed, but not in despair; persecuted, but not abandoned; struck down, but not destroyed. We always carry around in our body the death of Jesus, so that the life of Jesus may also be revealed in our body.[4]

Translation: You can knock down our castle walls, but you can't take the code found inside them. We are crushed almost beyond recognition—in Harry's case dead and sent to the morgue—but like Harry, and Shylock in Shakespeare's *The Merchant of Venice*, if you cut us, "Do we not bleed?"[5]

The answer isn't building walls; it's living by a code, and the code Jesus offers is simple—no rocks to carry up from the river, no mortar to mix. The code Jesus calls us to is not about building with stone but with love. As we stack love around ourselves, we find more protection than any wall can offer, more security than any moat will make, and more confidence than any we can create.

The castle Harry built with cement was impressive but not nearly as impressive as the things he built inside the hearts and minds of his Sunday school students. When Harry died, he handed the castle down to his knights who kept the castle open and continued to invite people inside. Millions of people have visited Chateau Laroche, and I'm betting many did some soul-searching as they stood within the walls. I was one of them. As I stood in the castle's great hall and looked at the code hanging high on one wall, I wondered what code I'd held high inside my life.

Like Harry, we choose to live by codes that will enable us to build things in our lives. I want to build my life in a way that invites people in, and I hope you do too. The world often takes a lot from us and leaves us with loss, and the emptiness can make us feel like our autopsies are the only things standing between us and the grave. No matter how empty you feel, you are not dead yet. You may have lost the love of your life. You may have lost a child. Maybe you lost yourself. Over the years, I've talked to people who have lost these things, and they all were confronted with a choice: Keep people out or let people in. Most of the regrets I've seen from people nearing the end of their lives happened because they built too many walls and kept too many people out.

When we build lives that let people in, we discover confidence much stronger than any found in stacked stones or cement. All the knights that guarded the castles Harry toured in

Europe are gone now. Harry is gone too. Walls protect only for a time. But a life lived by the code Jesus offers is a life of confidence that will last.

Do you want to change yourself? Do you want to change the world? Start with your heart and mind and the code Jesus offers. Jesus invites anyone who wants to live a life of confidence to join him in his life of love. It's a life mixed with love for God, ourselves, and our neighbors. It's the life God designed us for.

CHAPTER REFLECTION

The code you choose to live by will let you build more of what you want into your life. You will be tempted, however, to build in ways that keep people out of your life rather than inviting them in. Remember that you were made for relationships. And while relationships are always risky, they are always worth it. God wants you to invite people into your life who will help you flourish and grow in your love for him.

1. What external walls have let you down in your life? How have you kept people out of your life?
2. Name something you can do to let people in.
3. How are you living by the code Jesus offers? What might need to change so you can live more in line with him?

Remember that God intends you for a life mixed with love for God, yourself, and your neighbors. Ask God to help you invest more deeply in the lives of the people he has placed in your life. Pray that you will be able to embrace the help, encouragement, and guidance they offer you.

CHAPTER 10

Putting Doubt on a Diet

It's a foggy Monday morning, and I'm driving to a nursing home to visit two people who are dying. One has heart failure, the other has lung cancer. I'm visiting them because the bodies that have carried these people around for eighty or ninety years are giving out. Both are tired, both are scared, and both have doubts. As I think through the conversations ahead, I realize both people I'm going to see are hung up on things in their pasts. The fog is lifting as I pull into the driveway of the nursing home, and though I don't know it yet, I'm about to learn an invaluable lesson about doubt.

Vivian, in room 112, is anxious about her future because she feels unsettled about her past. She grew up in a rough home with a father who was quick to hit and easy to explode with anger. She's eighty-four now, her heart is failing, and she's on a special diet that has robbed her of the foods she likes to eat. The diet has depressed her, but her mind is still sharp and the light in her eyes speaks of untold goodness. Of the many stories Vivian has shared, there's one she has told me three times.

One night her father came home late, a strong smell of

bourbon on his breath and his hair-trigger temper primed to go off. As her father walked through the living room, he stepped on one of Vivian's toys. The pain in his foot set him off and sent his hand flying. He backhanded her hard enough to draw blood and break her nose. From how she winces when she tells the story, it must have hurt tremendously, but I can tell her father's hand didn't hurt nearly as much as his words.

Vivian says, "He told me, 'You'll never amount to nothin'. Your momma's a loser, your sister's a loser, and you're just like 'em!'" She shakes her head, disgust thick in her voice as she repeats her father's words.

"Did you believe him?" I ask.

"I believed him for many years."

"But you weren't nothing. Look at all you did with your life, all the people you helped."

"Yeah, I wanted to prove him wrong." She looks down at her hands and then says, "I spent my life proving him wrong." They are the right words, but I don't hear conviction in them, and I get the feeling Vivian isn't saying them to me; she's saying them to herself. I suspect this is a conversation she's had internally many times. As we talk in these final days of her life, this internal conversation is finding its external voice. Years have passed, but Vivian is still trying to convince herself what her father said that night isn't true.

"You proved him wrong," I say.

She hears me but is still looking at her hands.

"You proved him wrong," I say again, pausing between words, hoping my comment will reach her.

She looks up at me, but the light isn't in her eyes this time. This is a darker stare, one with aged anger.

"Then why am I still talking about him?" Vivian asks.

A conversation she had with her father more than seventy-five years ago, and she's still hung up on it. Her father's words cut so deeply into her past that they left seventy-five-year-old gouges in her self-esteem. Now she doubts. She doubts her heavenly Father will think she's good enough for heaven because her earthly father didn't think she was good enough for earth.

Many of us can relate to Vivian. Many of us are replaying one moment, one conversation that planted doubt so deep inside us we can't seem to let it go. The mother who made fun of our looks has caused us to doubt our beauty. The boss who fired us without cause has us doubting our skills. The spouse who left us for someone else has us doubting anyone else will love us.

Doubt lives deep. Like a wrong root twisted and planted thirsty, it grows on the sunlight of our past experiences at the expense of our self-esteem. As draining as doubt can be in our lives, there is an answer for doubters. A solution for the Vivians of the world that starts by understanding what doubt is and how it works.

DOUBT IS A BASEMENT DWELLER

In our first year of marriage, my wife and I moved into a rental house built in the early 1900s. The cracks in the windows let in hot air in the summer and cold air in the winter. In July, the smell of cat urine in one of the upstairs closets came alive and roamed the halls. The furnace barely took the chill out of the rooms in December, even though we stapled blankets over all the windows.

These issues would have been funny newlywed memories to look back on with laughter, but not the basement. The basement was no laughing matter.

In the basement, we discovered a smell much worse than

cat urine hanging so thick in the air you could taste it. The stone walls were a spooky backdrop of cracked bricks, and the floor was incomplete with sections of dirt that turned to mud when it rained.

We would have never ventured below the first floor, but the washer and dryer were down there, so every load of laundry forced us to endure the mud, the smell, and the spookiness.

My wife and I wondered if someone had been murdered down there. A dead body rotting in the basement would explain the smell, the cheap rent, and maybe the stains on the ground.

Our neighbors soon informed us the smell wasn't from a corpse.

It was from a goat.

The previous tenants had kept a goat who lived, ate, pooped, and smelled as a full-time basement resident for several years.

If you've ever wondered, when a goat is a previous tenant, he can pass his smell on to your clothes even though he doesn't live there anymore.

Smells have a way of attaching to memory, and even though we moved out of that house years ago, I can easily recall the smell of the goat.

Doubt is like a hungry goat in the basement of our minds. Doubt loves living down deep, attaching its stink to our memories, voraciously eating everything, and causing us to question ourselves and our capabilities. We know the hungry goat named doubt. Doubt loves to see us second-guess the decisions we've made or goals we've set. When we feel insecure about things we can't control, it's usually because doubt has escaped from the basement and is running free in our minds.

Doubt has a distinct voice. It's the voice baying when we take on the big assignment from our boss, "You don't have what it takes to deliver." It's the voice saying, "You'll never save

your marriage or never get out of debt." The voice whimper-
ing about all the questions you answered weakly in the job in-
terview after it's over.

Doubt enticingly acknowledges your good intentions, tells
you the goals you've set are reasonable, but then chips away at
your footing by reminding you of all the areas and ways your
plan will fail.

So what do we do with the goat living in our basement? Are
we doomed to live a life like Vivian's? A life where doubt both-
ers us now and every day until our final moments?

I found an answer as I talked with Vivian, one I think she
would want me to share with you.

Vivian's doctor prescribed a diet to limit certain foods so
fluid wouldn't put pressure on her heart. A diet that let Vivian's
heart beat again without restriction. The more I spoke with her,
the more I realized Vivian needed another diet, not for her
heart but for the goat living in her basement. Vivian had been
feeding the goat of doubt a steady diet and, in doing so, had
made him healthy. The healthy doubt goat was crowding out
her heart, confidence, and self-worth, and its smell was firmly
attached to many of Vivian's memories. Vivian needed to put
doubt on a diet, and we do too.

DOUBT ON A DIET

Doubt has two favorite foods, foods we would do well to keep
away from the goat. The first is our pasts.

OUR PASTS

Maybe you are like Vivian, and your parents or family repeatedly told you that you would never amount to anything. Being
told you aren't as good as the people around you, or that you'll

never succeed, can be quite a feast for doubt. We can't let the negative voices from our pasts play over and over in our minds. We need to press pause and ask ourselves two important questions. First, are the things being said about you true? Second, do you believe what's being said about you? If you answer yes to either question, you are preparing a meal for doubt, and likely on a daily basis. Doubt feeds on untruths and returns for second helpings when we believe them. Shining light on the lies will diminish our belief in them. It may take time, but the less we believe the untruths, the less doubt has to eat, and the less doubt consumes, the less he can interfere with your heartbeat.

OUR FAILURES

Doubt's second favorite food is our failures. I saw this food served up on a silver platter by the next patient I visited at the nursing home.

It's almost 12:30 as I enter room 128, Harold's room. Like Vivian, he's hung up on something in his past, but unlike Vivian, he's not the innocent party. Harold failed his family. He didn't hit them or hurt them; he left them. Harold inherited some money, and one night, after his family went to bed, he took the money and left.

"I left it all—my wife, my kids, my house, all of it," Harold told me. He spoke straight-faced without tears, but his pain was visible. The tears had dried up with time, but the tracks of regret and shame were still there. He knows he's nearing the end, and he has doubts. He doubts a heavenly Father will forgive him for being a lousy earthly father.

"I left my wife with no job, no money, and two small kids, just left them," Harold says. It takes Harold time to get the words out. There are spaces between every few words, pauses he uses to close his mouth and breathe through the clear tubing in his nose. He's rubbing the top of his head with one of his hands because he's frustrated. He wants to talk more but doesn't have the air.

In one of the pauses, I pick up the letter sitting on Harold's nightstand. We've read it many times. It's handwritten in blue ink, a short note he received from his wife in response to the letter I helped Harold write months ago. I read the last two sentences aloud.

"I forgive you, Harold. God has forgiven me, and I forgive you."

"You want me to read it again?" I ask.

Harold looks at me and nods; this time, I read the letter from start to finish.

I wish I could tell you Harold died free from his doubts. I wish I could tell you he forgave himself for the pain he caused his family, but that wasn't how Harold's story ended. His wife and daughters forgave him, and Jesus did, but Harold never forgave himself.

Each afternoon, Harold set the table with two places, one for himself and one for the goat. As painful as it was, Harold let doubt out of the basement and invited him to dine on his failure during each of his final days.

LIVING WITH DOUBT

Harold's doctor placed him on oxygen to deliver the air that was getting harder and harder to come by. The oxygen helped Harold, but only when he stopped talking. I found an answer for doubt in the silent spaces between Harold's words, and I think Harold would want me to share it with you. Most of us haven't left our families, but we've made mistakes that haunt us. Harold taught me that when forgiveness is given, doubt doesn't deserve any more of our words or any more of the air in our lungs.

After living in a house where the goat was a previous tenant, my wife and I decided to move to a better home. Had we not experienced the goat in the basement, we would never have moved to a much nicer place. It's the same for doubt. When we deal with doubt, we become better. Dealing with doubt strengthens faith.

Doubt isn't something we kick out; it's something we stop feeding and learn to live with. There will always be times when paranoia grows, self-worth decreases, and we prepare a meal of our pasts and failures for doubt to feed on. Anyone who has tried a diet knows there are times diets fail. For these times we have a cure. We don't have to let doubt run free on the main floor of our minds. The ultimate answer for doubt comes for all of us the same way it did for Harold and Vivian. The Savior.

I told Vivian and Harold that they were on hospice but that their doubts were too. Doubt will die with our last breaths, but we will breathe new air with new lungs in a place doubt does not exist. I'm pretty sure that when Jesus said he would prepare a place for us, he was talking about a place with no basements. I don't think there are basements in heaven, and even if there are, they aren't the kind you keep goats in. The Savior who waited for Vivian and Harold is waiting for you too. He knows all of your past and all of your failures. His opinion of you is unchanged, and his love is undiminished.

CHAPTER REFLECTION

Is there anything from your past you are serving up on a platter for the goat named doubt? Remember that doubt isn't something we kick out; it's something we stop feeding and learn to live with. You don't have to let doubt run free on the main floor of your mind. You have a Savior who not only knows your doubts but delights to help you overcome them.

1. List two things from your past you want to stop letting doubt eat. How are these things holding you back?
2. List two of your failures you want to take off doubt's plate. How might your life be different if you stopped fixating on these failures?
3. How might your life be different if you were able to live more consistently in the confidence of knowing God loves you?

Jesus knows your past—all of it: the good and bad, the wins and losses, the dreams and failures, the shame and success. Thank God for knowing everything about you and loving you still. Ask him to help you put doubt on a diet and live in the confidence of his love.

CHAPTER 11

Mirrors Are Not Standard Issue

Nevil's house was dark every time I visited. We'd sit in his living room, blankets over every window to keep out the sunlight and the lamp turned down to its lowest setting. When I'd knock on the door, Nevil would turn the knob just enough to unlatch it; that was my invitation to come in. He had cancer of the tongue, mouth, and throat, and it had taken part of his lower lip, part of his cheek, and almost all his self-esteem. There were no mirrors or shiny reflective surfaces in Nevil's house. He lived the life of a sheepish vampire, afraid he'd see his reflection or, worse, see the fear in someone else's face as they looked at him. Each time I pushed the door open and walked into Nevil's living room, I'd find him seated facing the wall. Nevil would turn his recliner so that when we talked, only his profile, the side less affected by cancer, could be seen.

"How are you today?" I asked.

"I'ne hine," Nevil said. He was saying, "I'm fine," but the words were difficult for him to form because of his cancer.

"What's your cat's name?" Aware of its long white hair, I expected Nevil to have named his cat Snowball or Whiskers.

"It's Rodrigo."

"That's an interesting name; where does it come from?"

"I named him after a parrot I had that died."

Maybe it was because he was more confident when he told jokes, but I understood that sentence very clearly.

I asked, "Who did you name your parrot after?"

"I named him after my guinea pig that died."

"He was named Rodrigo too?"

"He was an overly confident guinea pig. His name was Rod, but we thought he had a big ego, so we started calling him Rod Ego, and it turned into Rodrigo over time."

"That's funny," I said. "How is your ego these days?"

I'd been visiting for weeks but was still worried Nevil would not want to talk about his feelings. I was afraid he'd shut me out, but as I sat in the darkness of his living room, I was aware of two things. One, Nevil was hurting, and two, Nevil was dying.

He didn't shut me out. I was the only person Nevil had to talk with, and over the next three months, I discovered Nevil enjoyed the comedy in our conversations, but he craved the deeper connection just as much.

Nevil said, "I wish people were like Rodrigo. The cat, not the guinea pig. I don't wish anyone was dead."

"You mean you wish people didn't care about what you look like?"

"I'm the same person I was before the cancer, mostly. This has been the worst way to learn who your real friends are."

"Has that changed how you feel about yourself?"

"It did at first. Now I realize I was friends with a bunch of shallow people. I didn't change on the inside, and if they had liked me for the person I am, they'd still be my friends."

I understood most of what Nevil was saying, but he had to occasionally write a word on a yellow notepad, usually a word like *shallow*. Having to repeat himself a second or third time and still not be understood was frustrating for Nevil. Even if he slowed his speech or wrote words, it was still difficult for me to understand him at times, but I didn't have any problem understanding what he said next.

He said, "My friends are gone, and it's my fault." Rodrigo had climbed from Nevil's lap to his chest, and with the cat blocking my view of his jaw, Nevil turned his head in my direction and made eye contact with me. "I chose the friends I had. I accepted friendship at the surface level. I didn't get to know them, and they didn't get to know me, and now here I am."

It was a deep statement, and its depth was no doubt matched by the depth of Nevil's hurt. Near the end of his life, with a damaged mouth and lips, Nevil spoke clear wisdom. I learned a truth from Nevil, one I think he would want me to share with you. Shallow friendships will never carry us through deep hurts.

INNER IDENTITY

JJ has a big bark for a dog that looks more like an oversized hamster. JJ is a Maltese chin, a mixed breed of dog with partial Japanese origins. I'm guessing "Maltese chin" in Japanese means "mop-like," because JJ basically looks like a low-to-the-ground puff of fur. Unlike a mop, however, JJ is loud. Most people don't view JJ as an attack dog; her short, thin legs, fluffy fur, and small size usually make people want to cuddle instead of cringe. JJ would likely greet any burglar breaking into our house by rolling over onto her back and waiting for a belly rub.

JJ developed a deep hatred for large trucks soon after we brought her home to live with us, and while she isn't your typical attack dog, she is an attack dog.

When JJ hears the rough rumble and exhaust of a big box truck driving down our street, she matches the rumble with a growl of her own. Judging by how hard she claws at the door, JJ has every confidence she'll be successful in her mission to rid the world of big trucks. She hasn't had any major kills yet. She hasn't gone to battle with a single truck, but it's not for lack of trying.

During one of JJ's frantic outbursts, when the front door was the only thing standing in the way of destroying all big forms of transportation, I set a mirror on the ground in front of JJ's face. I reasoned if JJ saw how ridiculous she looked, teeth bared and acting crazy, she would realize how silly the attempted truck attacks were. However, JJ didn't acknowledge the duplicate dog staring back at her from the mirror. I thought it was odd, so I had each family member take a turn holding JJ's face an inch or two away from the large mirror in our front hallway. Instead of looking deeper into the glass, JJ looked past her reflection, refusing to acknowledge the identical image of herself. At first I thought all dogs couldn't see reflections, but I discovered our neighbor's dog, Stella, had no problem seeing herself. Stella loved looking at her reflection and even seemed to strike her best runway pose, choosing to look back at her reflection over her left shoulder.

"Is she afraid of her reflection?" my daughter asked.

"I don't think so," I said, because JJ wasn't looking away from her reflection; she wasn't afraid of standing nose to nose with a duplicate dog. Instead, JJ looked past her reflection, head held high and proud.

Finally I realized what was happening. She didn't recognize herself. The dog in the mirror didn't match JJ's self-image. When JJ looked in the mirror, she assumed she was looking at a little hamster-sized dog, and as a large attack dog, she couldn't be bothered by the lesser animal staring back at her.

I placed the mirror in front of JJ to show her what I thought was the truth, but it turns out JJ knew a truth about herself the mirror never could.

We all have a deeper identity, an inner courageous attack dog much more significant than any thin-mirrored reflection can reveal. When we believe who we are on the inside, no mirror can convince us of a lesser external identity. Shiny glass rectangles hanging on our walls don't get to decide our identities; only we have that power.

If JJ believed she was a tiny dog, she would lose her passion for attacking big box trucks. It's the same for us. When we let our mirrors define our identities, we squander true value for external fiction.

Don't get me wrong. We were created precisely with each part pinned and placed in position, so the image you see in your mirror each morning is a beautiful representation of your body, a body God made and values. The trouble starts when we give our mirrors the authority to tell us the ideal size, shape, and shade of skin that should be seen in our reflections.

I'm convinced this is why mirrors are not standard issue as part of our original design. God did not include them for good reason. Mirrors will diminish our self-esteem and rob us of our true identities if we let them.

We didn't realize this when we purchased our mirrors in the store, but they can be loud and sneaky ventriloquists. When I stand in front of one, it's the mirror speaking, but I hear my voice and the voice doesn't always say nice things. You've heard the mirror's voice; it likes to speak in the language of "I wish."

"I wish my nose was smaller."
"I wish I was taller."
"I wish my eyes were bluer, my clothes were newer."

"I wish my wrinkles were less, or my life wasn't such a
     mess."
"I wish my teeth were whiter and brighter and less yellow
     with plaque; I wish I had more hair on my head and less
     hair on my back; I wish I had more bulk on my arms
     and less bulk on my belly; I wish I could say no to
     doughnuts with jelly."
"I wish my skin was clearer."

Maybe what we should wish for are better mirrors.

If anyone takes advantage of mirrors, it's our inner critic.
Our inner critic likes to amplify outer insecurities internally
until the noise weaves into our self-thoughts. The inner critic
is the voice constantly comparing our reflections to the reflections of others and pointing out every area in which we haven't
measured up. The inner critic constantly speaks in "I'm not"
statements.

"I'm not good at directions."
"I'm not a good cook."
"I'm not successful."
"I'm not talented."
"I'm not coordinated."
"I'm not pretty."
"I'm not the smartest."
"I'm not well-liked."

We've given too much power to our mirrors, and our inner
critics are always present, waiting to take advantage of this.

I've discovered our mirrors have a warped view of the
world. Literally. Did you know that if a mirror is concave, bent
inward, even the slightest bit, it will make you appear taller
and thinner? Some clothing stores strategically place slightly

concave mirrors in their dressing rooms so we'll think we look taller and skinnier while trying on their clothes.

We learned a truth about mirrors at county fair fun houses long ago, one we need to remember: Mirrors cannot be trusted. We need to put mirrors in their place because they're inaccurate and are not authoritative.

When I google "mirror inspector," do you know what results come up? More mirrors. You'll find small mirrors on telescoping handles that allow mirrors to look in places they haven't before. I think it's a conspiracy put together by the mirror congress or whatever governing body governs the mirror society. When you google "mirror inspector," there's no result showing someone or some tool we can use to assess the quality of our mirrors' reflections. It seems inspecting mirrors for accuracy is an absurd thought.

And who came up with the seven years of bad luck if you break a mirror? I bet it was the mirrors.

On this side of Eden, we've installed mirrors everywhere— bathrooms, hallways, dining rooms, and even over the visors in our cars. We're determined to constantly re-inspect the creation God is already pleased with.

I want you to take a look at your mirror. Don't look in the mirror at your reflection. This time, turn the glass around and inspect the mirror instead of letting it inspect you.

I inspected our hallway mirror, and when I did, I discovered the truth about its capabilities. I realized we had brought the mirror into our home for decoration. The thick brown border of oak, the dark textured wood grain, the rich wrought iron, and the antique industrial look—we bought it because of the frame. Most mirrors are the same in the center; how you frame the glass makes the difference. As we assess ourselves, it's important to do so through the right frame. God provided the framework when he looked at us in the Garden of Eden and said his creation was very good. Our framework for looking at ourselves is God. The I Am. God said he is the "I Am." We need to walk away from "I wish" and "I'm not" and walk toward "I am." No one knows our true image better than I Am. I Am already inspected us, so it's time to stop re-inspecting ourselves with "I wish" and "I'm not." It's also no coincidence that the great I Am has given us power in the words "I am." If we want to change our identities, it starts with "I am" statements.

"I am a runner."
"I am a listener."
"I am a singer."
"I am a daughter."
"I am a mother."
"I am a hard worker."
"I am talented."
"I am worth dying for."

Speak your "I am" statements into your mirror if you want, but speak these statements into yourself to bring real change. We can use "I am" statements to inform ourselves of the people we want to be.

My friend Nevil discovered the value of his inner identity in his final days. Nevil had settled for shallow friendships in his life, friends who left when his outer appearance deteriorated, but even in this hardship, he realized his identity had nothing to do with his outward appearance. Unlike Nevil, we don't have to wait till our final days to discover the value of our inner identities. We can consult mirrors on things stuck in our teeth, but we shouldn't get stuck on anything a mirror says about our self-images. Mirrors are suitable for outward reflecting but not inward reflection. They are not an authority on what is good or bad about ourselves; that job belongs to us.

As I write this, it's Friday afternoon, and JJ is back to her mission of ridding the world of big box trucks. As I walked through the front hallway of our house, I realized the mirror I took down to show JJ her reflection was still sitting on the floor against the wall because the wire on the back came loose when I took it down. I picked up the dark oak-wood frame, reconnected the wire, and rehung the mirror. I stood in the hallway in front of the mirror and self-reflected.

When we don't like the look we see as we stand in front of a mirror, it's because we haven't recognized our true internal identities. God made us with inner identities more valuable than our outer appearance. Most of us have this backward and live lives directed by mirrors instead of identity. God didn't include any mirrors in our original equipment, and for good reason. The next time you stand in front of your mirror, don't give it too much power. We have self-images deeper than any thin reflective glass can reveal.

CHAPTER REFLECTION

When you look into the mirror, what do you see? I don't mean your specific physical appearance, but what do you see behind that? At the core, who are you? We are all tempted to compare ourselves unfavorably with the people around us who we assume are more capable, smarter, more accomplished, or more impressive. It's time to stop comparing yourself and see past your insecurities to the masterpiece God made you to be. God sees so much value in you, but more than that, he wants you to see your value too.

1. Do you have friends who have an accurate image of who you are? How might loving, supportive friends help us see ourselves more accurately?

2. Do you think you have an accurate self-image? What is one step you could take this week to see yourself more like God sees you?

3. God sees more value in you than you do. How should this truth change your posture?

Make a list of "I am" statements about yourself. Make sure these statements are accurate reflections and not distorted views from mirrors, other people, or circumstances. It may help to look at yourself from God's perspective.

CHAPTER 12

Our Flashlight Feature

I have a father who's great at fixing things. My dad often repaired a light or faucet or replaced a broken or failed car part during my childhood.

During these projects, he told me, "You hold the flashlight."

"Yes," I'd say, excited to be included in any project that involved working with my dad. With tools in hand, I'd follow Dad to whatever was broken. Sometimes the repair was electrical, requiring the power to be off and the house to be dark. Sometimes the repair was high in the ceiling or low behind a refrigerator or other appliance. Most of the time, the repair required me to hold the light with my arms fully extended over my head.

Car repairs called for me to balance on the front bumper while shining the light under the hood and down into the engine's belly.

My favorite time was crawling on our backs under the car to shine the light into the wires and mechanical guts.

My dad clearly defined my job; my job was to hold the light.

Early in my light-holding career, I eventually, either from

being off-balance, arms aching, or my mind wandering in a daydream, would let the beam of light drift from its intended target. My dad would say, "Hey, over here," and I would refocus and again shine the light onto the job.

My job hasn't changed a whole lot as I've grown up. I'm older now, but you can find me holding the light as my dad works on projects in my house or his, my car or his. It's funny. I always assumed I'd take over doing the actual work as I grew up and Dad would hold the light.

I've learned it doesn't work that way. I've learned a lot of things while holding the light.

I've learned about the job at hand. I can repair quite a few things in my house because I've seen the tasks completed. More importantly, I've learned about patience and persistence. I've learned that sometimes when your arms hurt and your attention drifts, it's time to refocus on the task and keep working.

I've learned about my dad and how great and solid and good his character is. Like when my dad worked late into the evening while it was snowing, lying on cold concrete to help a friend get his car working so he could make it to his job the next day. I've learned a lot while holding the light.

Recently I moved into a new house, and it was dark. I realized there was a broken light fixture, and I knew how to fix this because I had learned this repair while holding the light.

I felt a surge of emotion as I looked at my daughter and said, "You hold the flashlight."

She wasn't very good at it. I couldn't help but think my dad must have felt the same about me the first time I held the light for him.

It seems you never stop learning from your dad.

I started the lesson with my little girl, and I couldn't help but smile as I said to her for the first time, "Hey, over here."

OUR JOB IS TO HOLD THE LIGHT

The more we follow the Father, the more he reminds us that our job is holding the light. We think our job is to make repairs to ourselves and those around us, but this isn't the case. As we hold the light, we learn the responsibility of repairs remains with the Father.

God does the work.

God does the changing.

God does the fixing.

Our job is holding the light, not making the repair.

"But, Bryan, what about the things I need to change about myself?" you may ask.

We all have things we wish were different or better about ourselves. Self-improvement is a good and worthy goal, but the more we hold the light, the more we learn that God is the one who does the work of improving us. Many have wondered how this works. The apostle James wrote a letter to twelve different churches many years ago, and we have a copy of it in our Bibles today. James wrote, "My very dear friends, don't get thrown off course. Every desirable and beneficial gift comes out of heaven."[1]

Since all good is from God in heaven, becoming more like God is how change occurs within us. Still, with all our striving toward self-improvement, we must remember God loves us exactly as we are. God didn't send his Son to die for the person you can be or the person you are going to be. God sent Jesus for the person you were, and then he did something, something unexpected, something lasting and life-changing; he repaired you. God saw us in the darkness of our failures. He took his light to where we were broken and fixed us. Where we see broken fixtures and a fractured foundation, God sees a successful repair. Our "Hey, over here" moment is this. God isn't expecting us to make repairs—because he's already made them.

"Bryan, then why be better if God loves me as I am?" you may say. You aren't the first to ask this question. The early Christians in Rome had similar thoughts, so this time the apostle Paul wrote them a letter, and we have a copy of it today in our Bibles. Paul wrote,

> So, what do we do? Keep on sinning so God can keep on forgiving? I should hope not! If we've left the country where sin is sovereign, how can we still live in our old house there? Or didn't you realize we packed up and left there for good? That is what happened in baptism. When we went under the water, we left the old country of sin behind; when we came up out of the water, we entered into the new country of grace—a new life in a new land![2]

If you move out of a run-down shack and trade it for a brand-new house, you don't go back to make repairs to the run-down shack. Instead, you live a new life in the new house. Our old houses were death traps continually failing to live up to commandments and laws. We don't live in those houses anymore. We have moved into the house of grace. In the house of grace, no sin will undo the repair God has made in your life. Likewise, there is no repair we can make that will improve the work God has already done. We have been made holy. Have you ever considered yourself to be holy? If not, maybe this thought is a "Hey, over here" moment. In our new house, the question is not "What if I sin?" We will sin, but the repair God made inside us is bigger than our sin. In our new house, the question is not "Why should I strive to be better?" We are better. God's repair makes us better than any improvement we can complete ourselves. The real question for our lives in the new house of grace is "Why would I ever want to go back to the old way of living?" In the new house of grace, we are holding the light to remind ourselves we have left the old way of living and are instead becoming like God. In our new house of grace, we are holding the light to encourage others.

OUR JOB ISN'T REPAIRING OTHERS

Carl's house was enormous. I'd call it an old mansion from a bygone era that had been refurbished, except Carl's house wasn't refurbished. Carl was terminally ill, and so was his house. The city had threatened to condemn it, and it wasn't hard to see why. Four stories if you counted the basement, each unfit and dangerous. The carpet on the ground floor was so matted that it looked and felt like corkboard. The kitchen counter was cluttered with layer upon layer of appliances, leaving no visible counter space. The winding iron staircase off the back of the kitchen was missing a couple of steps, and it seemed someone wanted the stairs in the house to match because the steps to the basement were missing a couple of steps too. A hole in an upper level of the house let enough water in to make the ceiling on the main floor sag. Visible burn marks extended up from more than one of the electrical outlets in the living room, and the lights flickered when the wind blew.

The house was in bad shape, but the condition wasn't what made me dread my visits; it was the other residents. Mice, lots of them. They scattered when you walked into a room, could be heard in the walls and ceiling, and no doubt considered this house their home at least as much as Carl did.

In hospice, we use the phrase "self-determined life closure." It means each person is entitled to live their life as they see fit, right to the end. Though the city wanted to condemn his house, Carl's last wish was to die in it. Our hospice social worker, Carl's lawyer, and the city inspector reached a solution in multiple meetings. Carl's house would be inspected within three days. If we could show that the back room off the kitchen was safe, and if Carl agreed to live in only that room, then he could stay in the house and die there. The city inspector offered an extension of three months in exchange for the repairs; three months was likely more time than Carl had left to live.

Our hospice team meant well, but we overstepped our bounds. Our goal was to keep Carl in his house and grant his last wish. The part we missed was that Carl wanted to stay in his home only if the house was kept in its current condition. Still, the following Saturday, two social workers, a nurse, and I showed up with gloves, cleaning supplies, and a pickup truck, and we went to work.

The first mouse trap I set went off before I could take the second trap out of the packaging. We threw out an entire pickup truck's worth of old, broken appliances, removed the carpet, and scrubbed the newly exposed hardwood floors. We cleared a path to the door big enough for Carl's wheelchair and threw out dozens of fast-food bags piled in a corner. We tried to restore the back room to the standard we were accustomed to, a standard the city inspector was expecting. We cleaned in the name of good health, fewer germs, and safety till the house reached a level of cleanliness Carl hated.

In our haste to do what we thought was best for Carl, we neglected to do what Carl thought was best for Carl.

Like my well-intentioned hospice team, we assume we are meant to fix the broken people around us, but that job still belongs to our heavenly Father. Our definition of *broken* is not the same as the Father's, and if left to make the repairs, we'd focus on the things that mattered to us and miss the things that matter to the Father. Visiting people as a hospice chaplain, I've learned God hasn't equipped us to do the fixing.

We can bring happiness, but we can't make people happy.

We can bring emotional comfort but cannot take away emotional pain.

We can confront wrong, hate the sin, and love the sinner, but we cannot cure wrong, eliminate the sin, or restore the sinner.

God has given us a toolbox full of incredible tools, but even our best tools will not repair others; only God can do that. Many of us make the mistake of focusing on fixing the fallen instead of concentrating on caring for the crushed.

Trying to do the work ourselves involves setting down the flashlight and picking up a tool. When you set down the light, you're working in the dark. Selecting a tool in the dark seldom works, and searching for a tool we don't have won't work either. No, our job hasn't changed. We are to hold the light, bring love, and leave the repair work to the Father.

PICK UP THE TEMPO

One of the most iconic rides at Disney World is "It's a Small World." You've probably heard of it. Hundreds of millions have floated in little boats through scenes of singing animatronic characters. I bet you know the eponymous song that plays during the ride and could probably hum a few bars of it. The story you may not know is how Walt Disney made a final revision to the song, one that made the tune so catchy and unforgettable. Two brothers, Robert and Richard Sherman, composed the song for what they envisioned would be a slow boat ride. When Walt first rode the ride, the audio wasn't working, and the Sherman brothers sat beside Walt in the boat and sang the song live as he floated around the tiny track of water. Disney liked the song but had four words of advice for Richard and Robert. "Pick up the tempo," Walt said.

Many of us have drifted from light holding to repair making. If you are in this boat, you are not alone. When we find ourselves making repairs, we need a revision. We have the right song but not the right energy. Disney's four words are great advice for us today too.

We need to pick up the tempo. I'm not talking about the highway; we don't need more weight on our cars' accelerators. This change isn't about adding speed or doing life faster. The change I'm suggesting is an investment. An investment of time and energy and thoughtfulness. We need to pick up the tempo in our marriages, with our children, and in our relationships with God. These areas don't need more fixing. They need more light, and the only way to add light is to shine the light of the Father.

Perhaps your light-holding skills have become a little like the automated animatronic characters in the "Small World" ride. If your life's soundtrack has slowed to a ballad, do something about it. The people on the ride with us are counting on our voices as part of their soundtracks. Look at the people with you on the ride and bring the energy and enthusiasm only you can bring. Don't try to repair them; instead, introduce them to the One who makes repairs. As you do, you will rediscover the power found in doing the job God gave you: holding the light.

CHAPTER REFLECTION

Is there anyone in your life you are trying to fix? Perhaps we try to fix people because focusing on someone else's weaknesses makes us feel better about our strengths. Whatever the reason, we can ask ourselves some simple questions to determine if we've started trying to fix others instead of loving them.

1. Are you spending more time trying to change someone than you are on loving them? If so, how can you try more light holding and less repair making?
2. Is there a problem someone else is facing that you regret not solving? What is wrong with this way of thinking?
3. Are you feeling overwhelmed by someone else's problems? What is one way you can bring more of God's light and less of your repair making to the people around you?

Carrying our own burdens is hard enough. Carrying someone else's along with our own can be crippling. God calls us to care about the problems of others, but that does not mean fixing them. Remember that God is the one who fixes things; he is the one who redeems. Ask God to help you embrace his love and care. Ask him also to help you express that same love and care to people around you who are hurting.

CHAPTER 13

Our Check-Engine Light

The next time you have a newborn baby daughter, don't put her in the oven—it will make your wife a lot angrier than you think, even if you've left the oven door open and double-checked that the oven is off. Even if you've slid the oven rack out and made sure, for the third time, that the oven door stays open, your wife will still not like it.

When my daughter, Casey, was born, pictures by the photographer Anne Geddes were getting a lot of publicity.[1] Photos of babies in flowerpots and bowls of fruit and popping out of pumpkins were popular, and I thought it was something I could re-create. My wife didn't think it was funny when I texted her a picture I'd taken of our newborn daughter swaddled in a blanket and lying in a turkey pan on the oven rack with the door open. I intended to caption the photo "Fresh out of the oven."

Over a decade later, Maggie is still upset about it.

We need a warning system that tells us to pause and think through our actions, because even when our intentions are good, sometimes our ideas aren't. Knowing our decisions could endanger us, God wired us with a warning system. Even high-performance Lamborghinis need a mechanism to alert drivers when things aren't good with the machinery.

Think about the check-engine light on your car. It's the little orange light on the dashboard in the shape of an engine. It's lit when oil levels are low and temperatures tweak too high. It warns when spark plugs aren't sparking and flashes when filters aren't filtering.

When the check-engine light illuminates, it makes us ask questions. Is the car running smoothly? Does anything smell like it's burning? Is there smoke? In the worst cases, the check-engine light causes us to pull over to the side of the road and look under the hood.

We call the check-engine light God installed in us our conscience. Our consciences tell us when we need to slow down and pay more attention to how our machinery is operating, and in the worst cases, they warn us to pull over, look under the hood, and ask a few questions. My check-engine light was telling me something wasn't right about the photo op, and if I had paused, pulled over, and thought it through, I would not have put our baby in the oven.

One of my friends in college had a car with a check-engine light that was always on. When I rode with him, it seemed like the check-engine light was never enough of a warning for him, like it would have been better to have the word *Everything* flashing in red on his dashboard because everything was wrong with his car. The engine shuddered and smoked and made the worst noises, and the car was constantly overheating and leaving us stranded.

My friend put black electrical tape over the light to solve the check-engine light problem. All good, right? Not exactly. Ignoring the check-engine light in our cars isn't a good idea. Ignoring the check-engine light in ourselves is worse, but like my friend, we find pieces of black electrical tape to cover our warning lights. There are a thousand pieces of black tape, a thousand excuses we use when ignoring the warning of our consciences.

"Just this once; no one will know."

"Who's it going to hurt?"

"This company owes me the money anyway."

"It's not an affair; it's just a one-time thing."

"It's not really a lie."

"It's only one more drink; I can handle it."

Our electrical-tape excuses are convincing, at least to ourselves, but underneath the thin words, a flashing amber light blinks bright, warning of breakdown.

Humanity's check-engine light has been operational from the beginning, and from the beginning, we've been putting black tape over it so we could ignore the warnings.

Adam and Eve saw their check-engine lights when the snake tempted first Eve and ultimately Adam in the Garden of Eden. The amber warning light flashed because something in the serpent's slithery story wasn't right. I imagine Eve's conscience whispering for her to wait before she took the forbidden bite and Adam's amber light illuminating as Eve offered him the fruit. Can't you see the first couple's lights flashing and telling them to pull over? "Warning, Warning, Do Not Eat!"

We know how Adam and Eve's story ends, so it's worth asking, Was there something wrong with their equipment? Maybe a malfunction, something God missed in the prototype, or a bug in the beta version. It's worth knowing because our check-engine lights are the same make and model as Adam and Eve's. If we can understand what happened with Adam and Eve's warning lights, we can be more in tune with how our warning lights work.

No, Eve and Adam's equipment was in working order. The

black electrical tape for Adam and Eve was the thought of being like God, and they applied it over their check-engine lights and ignored the warning. The idea of being like God was so tempting Eve wasn't about to pull over and Adam wasn't about to stop her. The way Genesis 3 reads, Eve barely pushed back against the serpent's lie and Adam gave no objection to his wife either.[2] Eve's foot was still on the accelerator when she ran into the tree in the garden.

God didn't skimp on the warning system when he made us. Our check-engine light isn't a tiny amber-colored light on the dashboard; it's more like a full-on fire alarm. Our warning system is more extensive, like superhero, superpower big. Our engines run rough when we're doing something we know is wrong. Sweaty palms, quickened pulse, guilty expressions, red faces, high blood pressure, nervous speech, and sleepless nights are just a few of the dashboard danger signals. Our warning systems shout like a wailing siren when we do something dangerous. No, I'm convinced Adam and Eve's check-engine lights were working fine. Their problem was they didn't pull over.

Like slamming the snooze bar on our alarm clocks, mankind has overridden its consciences since the dawn of our existence. I've spoken with too many people confronting their mortality who have regrets because they've traded short-term gratification for long-term regret. It's not a good trade, but Adam and Eve weren't looking long term; they wanted to be like God and were convinced they could get there with a shortcut by eating one piece of free fruit. This side of Eden, Eve and Adam's mistake sounds simple, but most of us make the same deal when we face temptations like lust, greed, or envy. We put the electrical tape over the alert and fall for the lie. God didn't create us to be fulfilled by short-term gratification. There's no shortcut to having a better marriage, getting in shape, achieving more in our careers, getting out of debt, being a better mom, a better Christian, or a better student.

THE EXAMPLE

Years after Eve and Adam's experience, we get an up close look at another check-engine light, and this time it operates as intended. Knowing his execution was near, Jesus wished for a different outcome; anyone in his situation would. Still, God designed the conscience to speak up when we consider going against God's intended purposes for our lives.

When Jesus considered a path other than the cross, his check-engine light illuminated, and he pulled over. Jesus pulled over in Gethsemane's garden and stayed up all night praying. The garden was dark, the disciples were dozing, the crickets were chirping, and Jesus' amber check-engine light was flashing so brightly he was surprised his friends could sleep. Caught between the fear of dying a horrifying death and doing what his Father had sent him to do, Jesus asked God for another solution.

God was quiet. He didn't have to speak; he communicated through Jesus' amber warning light. Jesus asked if there was another way, and his warning system responded by sweating drops of blood. Thankfully for you and me, Jesus listened to his warning system, followed his Father's will, and saved humanity.

Sometimes it seems like God is quiet in our lives, but God speaks through our check-engine lights. Like Jesus, we often hear answers from God best when we pull over. We know Jesus heard God's answer in the garden because we hear him repeat the answer his conscience gave him when he said, "Not my will but yours." When we listen closely, we can hear our consciences saying things too. It doesn't have to be a Garden of Gethsemane. We can hear our warning systems in our offices, showers, or back porches.

HAMSTER DRINKING BINGE

Every morning I wonder if our hamster Dynasty Diamond (Dynasty Diamond is the name my daughter gave her, but we all call her Double D) goes on a nightly drinking binge. There's no alcohol in her water bottle, but from the looks of her cage each morning, you would think she spent most of the night drinking hamster beer from a secret hamster refrigerator buried beneath the cedar bedding. Every morning her cage is a disaster, the food dish is overturned, the running wheel slanted sideways, and the water bottle tipped over and empty.

Double D isn't drunk. It's a little sadder than that. At night you can hear the lid of her cage thump as she stands on top of her water bottle and pushes up with her tiny paws, trying to create an opening through which she can crawl to freedom. As Double D stands on top of the water bottle, her hamster arms can crack open the lid but can't open it wide enough to escape. After each lift of the lid, her arms wear out, and the lid crashes closed.

The thump of the lid can be heard for several hours each night till, finally, one attempt results in her losing her balance and tipping over the water bottle.

With the water bottle on the floor, there's nothing to stand on to reach the lid. The bigger issue for Double D is that the water she needs to live is now gone.

She's trapped in her cage but would rather die from thirst than give up a chance to escape.

We aren't all that different from Double D.

We choose our sin over salvation.

We bite the apple and lose paradise.

We see the check-engine light but keep driving.

The apostle Paul said it best when he wrote, "I decide not to do bad, but then I do it anyway."[3] We know what we're doing is wrong, but we keep driving till, like Double D, we wake to find our world a wreck. We need to learn to pull over.

Pull over before you wreck your marriage.

Pull over before your addiction causes your engine to overheat and explode.

Pull over before you drive headfirst into the oncoming traffic of a wrong decision.

Our check-engine light illuminates potential danger on the overnight business trip with a co-worker who asks to share a drink after the presentation. It blinks brightly in dark rooms when people are tempted to view pornography. It shouts out its warning to the sales rep who has a chance to get ahead of the competition if she's a little less honest.

Conscience weighs what we want on a scale alongside what is right and shows us what matters most. Conscience tells us the marriage is worth more than the one-night stand, sobriety is worth more than the drink, and holding your tongue is worth more than letting the insult fly.

Conscience weighs the short term with the long term, the immediate gratification against the better satisfaction. It's our consciences telling us not to eat the second doughnut or pick up the pack of cigarettes; it's our consciences warning us of things that turn into regret later.

CHAPTER REFLECTION

Did you catch the difference between Adam and Eve's warning lights and Jesus'? Jesus turns off the engine, pulls over in the garden, and receives answers. Instead of pulling over, Eve picked up a passenger, one all too willing because he has ignored his check-engine light too. Eve gave Adam the fruit and pressed the accelerator to the floor. Adam and Eve's warning lights were working fine, but like any other warning system, it helps only if the people being alerted listen and respond.

Think of a time your check-engine light was on.

1. In what ways did it warn you? What caused it to go off?
2. Have you ever had regret for not listening to your check-engine light? How so?
3. What are ways we can listen more closely to our check-engine lights? How might doing so help you grow in your relationship with God?

Your conscience is designed not to hold you back but to protect you so that you can go forward with confidence and joy. Take a moment and thank God for a time he used your conscience to guide and protect you. Ask him to help you listen to your conscience as a means to learn and grow.

CHAPTER 14

Our Lifesaving Component

When you wake up to go running on an old volcano, it's okay to be a little late.

My family was vacationing at a resort on top of Mammoth Mountain in California. The vacation lodge sits on top of a dormant volcano, one well known for its ski slopes in the winter. We were there in July to hike the trails and unplug from city life. Mammoth is part of the Inyo National Forest, and in every direction, you see a painting of blues, greens, and rugged browns. The crystal-blue waters of the lake combine with an endless expanse of blue sky, and together they weave a magical spell on you till you promise yourself you'll return to this spot as often as possible. I felt like my eyes drank in the sky and my lungs breathed in the mountains, leaving me with a fullness unparalleled by any food or beverage.

Mammoth mornings call you from your covers; every bird, every tree, and even the sunlight is so happy to be there they can't wait to get started. Running and hiking trails entwined with tree lines wrap around the mountains, and you can't wait to get out on them to do more tasting of all nature has to offer.

My wife, who already likes to be out running before the rest of the family wakes up, heard the morning call. For most of us, 5:00 A.M. is prime snooze-button time, but it's the start of my wife's recharging, and Mammoth was multiplying the recharge for Maggie.

Maggie has a shirt that reads, "Not Running Sucks." When she wears her shirt, she means it.

Maggie craves the alone time of early hours, but this morning she was late for her run because she couldn't find her running shoes and, though she didn't know it at the time, being late would result in not being alone on the trail. If Maggie had known what awaited her on the trail, she would have skipped the run, put on her "Not Running Sucks" shirt, and been content. This morning on Mammoth Mountain, running late may have saved her life.

"Have you seen my shoes?" she asked.

The room was dark, and Maggie was unzipping side pockets and rummaging through open suitcases.

"You're asking me?" My pillow muffled half the words. "Usually, I'm asking you where the things I've misplaced are, not the other way around."

Maggie was picking up the bedspread that hung off the end of the bed, looking under the blankets and behind the suitcases leaning against the wall. She was becoming frustrated, feeling the Mammoth morning slipping away as the clock ticked closer to the rest of the world waking.

We often don't recognize the moments that save our lives—the few extra minutes spent searching for shoes or seconds wondering where we put our wallets.

By the time Maggie got out on the trail, the sun was peeking through the tall pines.

The running trails at Mammoth parallel the road and, in several places, pass under the pavement through metal culverts road crews have converted into tunnels. The tunnels are large enough to stand in but not roomy by any stretch. There's little light in the tunnels at daybreak, so they are dark and would have been darker had Maggie found her shoes a few minutes sooner.

Maggie had been on the trail for almost two miles when she ran into a tunnel, slowing slightly to let her eyes adjust to the dim light. When she ran out the other side, her shoes skidded to a stop in the gravel. A large bear was only a few feet in front of her in the center of the trail. Maggie froze, but the bear did not. The bear kept walking directly toward Maggie, never slowing. Maggie panicked, and as a runner, she did the thing she does naturally, the thing she had gotten up at 5:00 A.M. to do: She ran.

They say the worst thing you can do is run from a bear once it sees you, but Maggie ran and kept running; she ran as a reflex of fear, heart pounding and fearful to look behind herself. When she finally looked over her shoulder, she saw the bear had followed her but was now uninterested and walking off the trail into the woods.

If Maggie had found her shoes a little sooner, she may have met the bear head-on in the tunnel in the dark.

MEETING THE BEAR IN THE TUNNEL

We all have bears waiting for us up ahead in the tunnels of our future, and it's hard to be confident in life when putting on our shoes a minute earlier or later can carry us to safety or catastrophe. Still, like the rule about not running from a bear, we understand we can't run from our future because it waits for us up ahead in places we can't see.

I can't help but think of the man who overslept and missed

his flight only to watch in horror as the plane he should have been on flew into the Twin Towers. I'm sure some people missed their seats on the *Titanic* and learned later it sank. I read about a boy living in Nagasaki, Japan, who had to do his paper route rather than swim with friends. The choice between swimming and delivering newspapers was the choice between surviving a nuclear bomb or not. These are all examples of people like Maggie who somehow missed running into the bear in the tunnel.

What about the people who stayed in Nagasaki, those who went down with the *Titanic,* and those on the 9/11 flights? If God is saving us while we're putting on our shoes, what about the people who do run into the bear while running through the tunnel? How can God watch out for all of us when what's best for one may not be good for another? When God looks down on the farmer who prays for rain and the young woman who prays for sunshine on the same day because it's the day of her wedding, how does he choose if rain should fall or not?

Does God turn his back on the people who make bad decisions? The woman who presses the accelerator when the traffic light turns yellow is killed by a car that hits her as she drives through the intersection. The husband who smoked the one additional cigarette that caused his cancer, or the teenager who decided to swim across the river but misjudged the current and drowned.

The conundrum is clear—how could God give us free will and still save us from our choices? How did God let Adam and Eve choose to eat the forbidden fruit but destine the rest of us for lives that end in death?

There's an answer. Embedded in our design is a remedy for the riddle.

When God formed us, he fell in love with his creation.

Love was there in the ether of the Garden of Eden, in the

air, as God stooped down and scooped up handfuls of dirt to make us. God breathed a spark of himself into us, and as it burned from an ember to a glow, God was grinning because he saw it was good.

Can you picture the Creator smiling as he made us? God was smiling because he fell in love with what he had made. God used the dirt of the earth and his breath, but he mixed one additional ingredient into our makeup—love. When God's love became a part of us, it added a lifesaving ingredient to who we are. God embedded his love in us as a flotation device; a part of our anatomy now makes us valuable. This love motivates God to offer us salvation.

I don't claim to understand why, but God loves his creation so much that he lets us choose our futures and then saves us from the fates we've chosen.

He could have started over, using the same voice he used to make us. When humans messed up, God could have wiped the timeline clean. "Let there be dark" could have just as easily echoed from God's lips, and the sum of all he made would have been washed blank. When I wonder why God didn't start over, I realize love caused him to choose another way. God's love is an inner flotation device deep inside us, constantly keeping us afloat in a sea of destined dangers. While we're still searching for our shoes, God is saving our lives, and the absolute underlying truth is God knows every day some of us miss meeting the bear by minutes or seconds, but the miss is temporary. We will all meet the bear head-on in the tunnel eventually. Adam and Eve's choice secured our mortality, but God's love promised the cross so that humanity's final moment would not be the minute we left the Garden of Eden.

THE SOUND OF FORGIVENESS

There's a story in the Bible about a woman caught having an affair.[1] Malicious people tore her from her lover's arms and pushed her to stand before Jesus. I wonder what it was like to stand with a crowd of people watching, her shame a spectacle, her moral failure on display. As the story goes, the woman's accusers shout angrily, saying she broke the law and must die. Attention turns to Jesus, all eyes waiting, watching to see how he will answer.

Jesus' response reminds me of when God made us. He stooped down and wrote in the dirt. I can't help but wonder if Jesus remembered his Father stooping down and scooping up ground to make us, to make the people who were shouting at him now. We don't know what Jesus was writing with his fingers, but maybe it was a simple list of ingredients because one ingredient was missing in this story.

Dirt?

No, dirt was there; he was writing in it.

God?

He was there stooping down in the crowd's presence. But where was the love?

Jesus saw the accusers standing with stones in their hands, blind to God's love for this woman he created. Jesus answers this mob by revealing the missing ingredient. He reminds the crowd there is love for this woman. Every person in the crowd had made mistakes; any one of them could easily be standing where the woman was now. Jesus reminds these people that the answer to bad choices isn't stones, and it isn't death.

The answer to bad choices is love.

Jesus looked at this woman and saw the embedded flotation device inside her, the beacon God wired her with, constantly compelling our Creator to save us.

We struggle to recognize the flotation device found in our inner equipment. God saves us, no strings attached, nothing to earn, no evaluation of performance needed. God keeps us because he loves us.

What happens next in the story isn't recorded in the Bible, but I know it occurred.

There's a sound coming from the crowd, a sound Jesus heard, a sound the woman heard.

We can't hear it in the printed version of our Bibles, but it happened.

It's the sound of the stones as they fell from the hands of the people holding them and hit the ground.

There was a thud as each accuser dropped their accusations. Each stone dropped was the drumbeat of freedom for this woman.

Thump. The sound of the woman's life saved.

Thump. The sound of the woman's pardon echoing off the walls of the tunnel, the sound of the bear held at bay for another day.

Thump. The sound of the Creator returning love to the mixture and makeup of his creation.

Accusations make lousy stones when there are no accusers to throw them. The woman heard the thump as each stone dropped, and she was left standing in a field littered with accusations that were now lifeless on the ground.

Like the woman, we've condemned ourselves with the choices we've made. We're caught in the act of bad things all the time, and our terrible decisions gather like a crowd of people, all armed with consequences that will kill us. Daily, we find ourselves in situations where we've removed love from the mixture the Creator's made.

So God, knowing our fate again, stoops down to the dirt. God sends his Son to the dirt this time, so the stones of our bad decisions, the stones destined to kill us, will be dropped for eternity.

Many of us still desperately need to hear those stones hitting the ground.

We need to hear the sound of our mistakes hitting the ground.

We need to hear the sound of our grudges hitting the ground, and we need to hear the sound of all the doubts we've had in ourselves drop to the ground in a reverberating *thump* of freedom.

Love saves us when no saving is deserved. There is love for the alcoholic who received his five-year chip but fell off the wagon again. There is love for the church leader caught in a lie and for the spouse who wasn't faithful. For the man who stole something and the woman who treated someone horribly, the disrespectful daughter and the son filled with hate. We might find it hard to love all of these, but God loves them.

It turns out Maggie's shirt is right: Not running sucks. We should run.

We should run the best race we can in this life. We can run knowing that no matter if we meet the bear sooner or later, God loves us so much that he sent his Son to the dirt to save us. While you and I are searching for our shoes, God is saving us. The lifesaving flotation device embedded inside of us is God's love.

CHAPTER REFLECTION

God fell in love with you, his creation, and his love continues to save us and forgive us from our pasts. Still, too many of us haven't forgiven ourselves. We may never face physical stoning like the woman in Jesus' time who was caught in adultery, but we do face emotional and mental stoning. Some of us pick up stones daily to throw at ourselves, and the weight of carrying them around, and the threat of throwing them, is not helpful or healthy. We need to hear the sound of those stones hitting the ground.

1. What past mistakes or sins are you arming yourself against? Isolate one in your mind. What will it take for you to drop that stone?
2. Is there a grudge you are stoning yourself with? Maybe a previous employer who treated you badly, a family member you disagreed with, or someone you used to call friend who now you never call.
3. Why is it so hard to forgive yourself? What will it take for you to drop those stones?

Whether you are carrying around doubts or insecurities, the solution is the same. It's time to stop picking up those stones and start believing in yourself the way God believes in you.

CHAPTER 15

Quiet Oil

The next time you must choose between eating an apple or a Reese's Peanut Butter Cup, remember what happened with Eve. An apple a day may keep the doctor away, but it may also sentence all humans to weed our gardens for life.

We may be eating Reese's Peanut Butter Cups for the good of all of humanity.

I'm doing my part.

Did you ever wonder why God created us with a happy response to chocolate? Our design is so intricate we have a chocolate response, a chemical reaction set into motion by chocolate as part of our standard-issue factory-installed components.

Chocolate has intrinsic ingredients that trigger our neurotransmitters. We crave chocolate because when we eat it (especially Reese's Peanut Butter Cups, in my case), our bodies release serotonin and dopamine. Those neurotransmitters lower stress and create a pleasurable sensation in our brains. As part of our high-performance equipment, God created us with numerous response components, just like our chocolate response, all of them designed for us to experience happiness.

Even though God removed humans from the paradise he created for us, our original response components remain unchanged. One component, in particular, is essential for us to uncover and put into use today; it's our quiet-response component.

Just as he created our chocolate response, God designed us with a quiet response. Quiet is the oil that keeps our equipment from overheating. You may not be a person who enjoys quiet; some of us don't, but we have a component inside us that needs a dose of quiet now and then to keep our engines working correctly. I first learned the value of quiet in a small blue trailer in Ohio.

WARNING DRIPS

When I was single, I lived in a blue trailer with thin ceilings, thinner walls, and a homemade brick sidewalk that led your feet to the front door.

One muggy midnight, a thunderstorm with big noise and bigger wind blew across the trailer. The storm snapped trees and stole sleep before finally subsiding in the early hours of the morning. In the silence, I found a peaceful quiet perfect for my pillow and fell into a deep sleep. It was in this silence that I heard the sound: *drip*.

I pretended to ignore it, not wanting to wake, but the sound persisted.

My body wanted to sleep, but my brain wanted to know what the sound was.

Drip went the sound again.

Not fast drips, but slow drips with heavy spaces of silence between each one.

My brain asked my ears what they were hearing; was it a drip or a tapping sound?

Again, the sound. *Drip.*

Definitely a drip.

I pushed a heavy foot from under my covers and let it fall to find the floor, the rest of me frozen in place in protest. *Drip.*

My brain, now fully awake and processing, directed my feet out of my bedroom. Nothing in the kitchen.

No sounds in the living room either.

Drip.

Rubbing my eyes and yawning, I shuffled across the carpet into the office. My eyes scanned the room. Was the floor wet in the corner?

Yes, there was a puddle and a small area of standing water.

Was that a broken plate on the floor beside the puddle?

A few steps closer. No, not a plate, a broken ceiling tile.

I straddled the puddle and bent to pick up ceiling pieces. As I bent over, a fat drop of water landed on the back of my head. *Drip.*

That was the sound I'd been hearing; I recognized it as it thumped the back of my head, the fat drop splitting in two and running down both sides of my face.

Wiping the water away, I looked up.

Water leaking through the roof had pooled in the lining between the ceiling and the rafters. The plastic sagging from the water had broken the ceiling tile and made a dangling pocket of plastic now hanging from the top, directly over my head.

As I looked up, I found a huge coiled snake two inches from my face—a very big snake that evidently had been living in my ceiling for quite some time. I'm not sure if the water's cold temperature had chilled this snake, keeping it coiled in the plastic lining that now hung down at eye level. I know the snake was so close to my face that I could have stuck out my tongue and touched it. I hate even the smallest snakes, and from my Bible reading, I have rightly deduced God does not want these creatures at eye level with humans. I stood petrified, watching through the clear plastic as the snake's large head, about the size of the palm of my hand, moved.

I didn't hesitate.

I did the only thing I knew to do at that moment.

I screamed like a frightened child.

If it weren't for the quiet, I might not have learned about the snake in the ceiling.

We can only hear the warning drips of destined dangers if we step out of the noise of our everyday distractions. The quiet at the blue trailer came in the calm after a big storm, and while this is often the case, we don't have to wait for storms to pass to experience quiet moments. We can create them.

Creating quiet is like digging for treasure; good treasure hunters carry pickaxes to dig in places with the hardest ground. The hard ground for us is our calendars and maybe our alarm clocks. Pick up your pickax and create some quiet. Carve out a time quiet enough and long enough to run a self-diagnostic test on your internal equipment. When our computers have trouble, we restart, reboot, cut the power for a few seconds, and start over. The quiet you create is your reboot. When we're exhausted, the answer isn't quitting, it's quiet.

LISTENING FOR THE MAKER

Quiet connects us with the Maker. God designed our internal parts for the Garden of Eden, an environment quieter than most of the settings we live and work in today. In humankind's first days, God walked through the garden and looked for

Adam and Eve so he could talk with them. There was no email, morning commute, or YouTube in Eden. God created a garden where we could listen for him as he approached.

God is walking and talking in our world today, but with all the noise around us, it's often hard to hear his footsteps or find his voice. The noise of our world has disrupted the order of Eden, but some of Eden's order can be restored in our quiet times as we place ourselves where we can hear God speak. Don't worry—the quiet I'm talking about isn't a monthlong monastery vow of silence high in the mountains. Quiet is like oil to our machinery; when using oil, typically, only a drop or two is needed. A drop or two of quiet applied to the squeaks of your hinges will make opening doors in your life a little easier.

THE GOD OF ALL BREATHS

Today I work for hospitals, but before earning an MBA from ITT Tech and certifications from Harvard, I spent more than a decade as a hospice chaplain, sitting at the bedside of people breathing their last breaths.

You gain a bigger understanding as you sit with people and pray in those last moments.

Near the end, when each breath is precious, people choose their words carefully and speak less. In the quiet spaces where no words are spoken, we discover a complex God in simple silences.

God is not only the creator; he's not just the God of first breaths; he's the sustainer.

He is the God of second, third, fourth, and four millionth breaths. Our breathing is a continual reminder of a God with us from our first breath and even beyond our last. There is a message of mercy and grace in our breathing equipment. God is not just the God of second chances; he's the God of third, fourth, and tenth chances.

When we find God in every breath, we discover a God who gives out mercy and grace as often and as richly as he gives the air around us.

We can't un-bite the apple, but we can reclaim Eden's order as we rediscover our breath in quiet times. The God who chose to make the universe out of nothing and us out of his breath is still present and able to provide everything we need.

As we breathe, we imitate the creation by drawing in the air's chaos around us and organizing it so oxygen is harnessed and put to work. A reorganizing quiet found in our breathing reveals the purpose of God's order amid the world's chaos. I know it sounds good and seems complicated (I get it), but remember, the hardest part of finding quiet is in carving out moments from our busy schedules.

As I looked up at the snake hanging from my ceiling, only a thin layer of plastic separated me from it. A phone call produced a helpful neighbor who sliced through the thin plastic and disposed of the problem. Sometimes the thinnest of barriers stands between our current stress and a solution. We need quiet to identify the problem, to filter out the trivial from the vitally important.

God can speak through earthquakes or fire, and he's rebuked a storm or two, but he's mostly known for speaking in whispers.

I'm not asking you to carve out days, weeks, or months—just moments. When the debates about minor points of religion become louder than our conversations about Jesus, we need to create moments quiet. We need to seek moments of quiet to hear God approaching so we can listen to his voice over the noise of our own.

We need to claim quiet so we can hear the name of the Creator in our lives entering and exiting our lungs. Quiet lets us catch our breath. When we find quiet, we press the mute button on the world around us, and if we listen long enough, we can hear the one voice we need to hear in the newfound silence.

I'm not talking about a mystical, hocus-pocus trance. Far from it. The quiet I'm talking about dampens the noise around you, letting you listen to your internal workings. Quiet enables us to hear our breath. Quiet is waiting to be discovered by you, and there are simple steps we can take to claim it.

PICK PLACES

A whispering waterfall would be lovely, but let's be realistic. Nature can be a beautiful backdrop for finding the moments we need, but nature's not always accessible in our daily routines. Put a chair in your walk-in closet, spend a few moments with your office door closed and phone on mute, or park your car in a secluded spot after dropping the kids off at school. The place doesn't have to be a scene out of *National Geographic;* God made those places, but he made the ground your garage is built on, too, and that spot may be the ground you choose to claim in the name of quiet.

FIND TIME

Remember, we're carving moments, not months. Mark it on your wall calendar, set an alarm, or enter it as an appointment in Outlook. Make a habit of an early morning walk. The battle with the snooze button can feel big, but these moments will be worth it over time.

Take small sips and great gulps.

We aren't seeking extended stays in a monastery, but we must claim quiet in available quantities. Sometimes we can claim five minutes and sometimes fifty-five. To a soul thirsty for time with the Savior, we'll find quenching in both small sips and great gulps. Drink in time when you can but keep coming back to fill your cup. Quiet waits in sunlit nooks over morning coffee and in between squeaks of the front porch swing as evening falls.

You can find quiet on your knees, pulling weeds in your garden, or as you sit on your favorite park bench. Quiet moments wait in the prayer corner of our closets, on a pier overlooking the ocean, or during the morning commute with only the sound of our tires on the road. There's a quiet waiting just before sunrise, and we can find it when we choose to overpower our snooze buttons.

As you claim quiet moments, you will hear the footsteps of the Maker approaching. He's been there all along, waiting for an opportunity to speak with you.

CHAPTER REFLECTION

Where do you go to recharge? Garden, hiking trail, coffee shop, bookstore, your office, porch swing? During times we feel like quitting, escaping to these places for a respite can help us re-center and find a new gear. When life is off balance, we need to re-center, but the time we need is hard to find so we must make it. May I make a few suggestions?

1. Pick up your pickax. Where can you carve out a few moments for yourself? How might doing so help you reset?
2. Claim quiet moments for yourself and for prayer. Do this consistently in the same place at the same time and see if God meets you there. How might taking time to pray change your perspective about frustrations, stress, or disappointment?

3. Remember that you can pray anywhere at any time. How might you recognize God's presence in things you do each week?

Quiet is waiting to be discovered by you, and there are steps you can take to claim it. Make a simple plan to create quiet this week in order to meet with God. Commit this plan to God today.

CHAPTER 16

Sawhorses

bid on a boat at an auction and won—a sixteen-foot rowing scull, long and thin with antique wooden oars. At $895, I felt like I had won the lottery because I'd seen boats like this with much higher price tags. But as I was bidding, I knew I was buying "as is." I hadn't seen the boat with my own eyes, but I had faith I could fix anything needing repair with the help of a higher power, YouTube. What else do you need besides faith and YouTube? My logic? Faith is believing in things unseen, and YouTube is how you fix those unseen things.

I got the boat home and discovered three cracks that would leak water. I was still enthusiastic because I found a fiberglass repair video on, yep, YouTube. YouTube wasn't my only help, though. When my daughter saw the boat, she was more excited about making the repairs than I was.

"Can I help you, please, Dad, please?"

Casey was only eleven then, but she knew as much about boat repair as I did, so I put her to work. I handed Casey the electric sander and told her to smooth out the area around the cracks.

"Dad, the bottom of the boat is getting hot," Casey said, holding the electric sander over the boat's hull.

"That's great, dear," I said, not taking my eyes off the video I was watching.

I should have paid attention to this comment.

I should have responded more quickly to the smell of smoke.

When I looked at Casey's work, a plume of blue smoke was billowing from underneath the sander. Casey had sanded clean through the hull, making not a crack but a sander-sized hole.

As I looked at the lack of progress on the first three cracks and considered the new hole, I could see the boat sinking, and to be honest, my enthusiasm for this project was sinking too.

Still, I started making repairs. I ordered the fiberglass repair kit, but delivery would take two weeks. I ordered paint for the scratches, but it would take four weeks for that to be delivered. When I bid on the boat, I envisioned rowing out into open water, gliding on the surface of an enormous lake on a crisp morning. Instead, I had a boat with a hull that looked like Swiss cheese, stuck in my garage, upside down, and balanced between two sawhorses.

Can you relate? Have you ever felt you were destined for open waters only to find what you thought was seaworthy was actually sinkable? We all endure our fair share of holes and cracks that submerge our confidence and steal our purpose.

If you've felt this way, it's okay. When we lack the confidence for the bigger bodies of water waiting in our future, God reserves time for us on his sawhorses. He has the material for your patches and the paint for your scratches. Jesus works in the garage, too, helping his Father, and he's ready with a repair for each of our setbacks. Jesus is the alpha and omega, and in the ancient Greek text, that roughly translates to "better than YouTube." Jesus paid a great deal more for us than I paid for my boat, but like me, he has every intention of helping us get back into the water again. God has reserved people, places, parts, tools, techniques, and time as he provides the precise repair you need.

Chances are someone reading this is on the sawhorses now.

You've prayed for a better job but are stuck in the one you have.

You've prayed for a mate but are still sleeping alone.

You've prayed for a baby, but the pregnancy tests continue to read negative.

We all spend time on the sawhorses—waiting for things to improve and our circumstances to change. Isaiah 40 tells us as we wait, we will "spread [our] wings and soar like eagles" and find new strength to lift us out of our current challenges.[1] If I'm being honest, Isaiah's words feel frustrating, with wings far off and time on the sawhorses crawling at a snail's pace. In the middle of our "broken down," it can be hard to believe in a time of soaring, and new strength can feel far away when our tiredness is close and deep. I've realized something about this scripture. We've been reading it upside down. Isaiah's words seem upside down from our vantage point, but doesn't that make sense? If we are upside down and stretched across God's sawhorses, Isaiah's words are right side up. The words only feel upside down because we are upside down. It's hard to believe in our ability to soar because we've forgotten that soaring comes only after we are given fresh strength. Take a look at this familiar verse again, but as you read the words, imagine yourself not just in a posture of waiting but in one where God is working, fixing, and equipping you. Imagine a God of action who is about to flip you over and turn you loose upon the world, fully repaired and ready to go.

But those who wait upon God get fresh strength.
They spread their wings and soar like eagles,

They run and don't get tired,
   they walk and don't lag behind.[2]

Here are words to help us turn our perspective from upside down to right side up.

WHILE WE WAIT, GOD WORKS

As we wait, God removes the tools from our hands and goes to work. If our strength were enough, we'd have already accomplished the tasks we were trying to tackle. We must sit until someone else can do the work. When we wait, we give up the efforts that aren't working and place ourselves in the hands of the One who can do the work.

WHILE WE REST, GOD REVIVES

Isaiah tells us we find new strength because waiting is rest. Waiting on God not only lets him go to work but it lets us recover from the exhaustion of working on problems we were not able to solve. Waiting is hard because rest doesn't feel right if you haven't accomplished or finished what's in front of you. It's okay. While we rest, God does the rest.

WAITING TURNS CONVALESCING INTO CONDITIONING

No offense to Isaiah, but running and not growing tired isn't an elusive science. We learn to run marathons by first learning to run one mile well. Do you dream of traveling the world and teaching people about God? God may want you to start by teaching Sunday school where you are. He's not closing the door to the bigger dream. He's conditioning you for its success. Waiting can be hard when we try to run a marathon before mastering the mile. In your time of waiting, look for short runs you can master.

WAITING MONITORS MOTIVES

An honest look during a time of waiting can reveal good intentions but wrong motives. Maybe we want to impact the world for God, but we want to accomplish this through our fame on social media. Impacting the world for God is good, but God may not feel quite as fantastic about fame. Waiting can match motives to intentions. An honest look during a time of waiting can reveal a good long-term vision but a short-term dedication. We want to write a book that will help people but burn out after writing a couple of chapters. God uses time on the sawhorses to help us determine if what we want is worth the wait. Waiting can build long-term commitment to match our long-term visions.

WHILE WE WAIT, WE GET TO KNOW GOD

We say we want to know God but don't recognize waiting as an opportunity for this to happen. Waiting is an opportunity to align our wills with his and to understand who God is and what his vision means for our lives.

WAITING IS PRESCRIBED

We live in a society that doesn't want to wait. We tap our feet in front of microwaves, get angry at traffic lights, and expect our coffee as soon as our thumbs hit "submit" on the mobile Starbucks app. We don't like to wait, but we've seen this model before. When we are sick, we go to a doctor. But going to the doctor always involves waiting. Doctors have rooms just for waiting and name them accordingly. And once we are out of the big waiting room, we are taken to smaller, colder rooms so we can do more waiting with fewer clothes. We wait to be examined for prescriptions, tests, and healing. We need the same expectation of God that we have of our doctors. We endure waiting on our doctors because we trust they've seen what we are suffering from before. We trust our doctors have the knowledge, skill, and answers we need. We need to trust that God has the same. Make an appointment with the Great Physician. While in the waiting room, peruse the reading material he's left for you. As he looks at X-rays and determines the best course of treatment, be assured that the waiting is worth it.

GOD WILL ADD THE STRINGS

My friend Bob always wanted to build a guitar. When he was younger, he found a skilled craftsman who showed him how to cut out the wooden pieces, then shape, sand, and assemble them into a beautiful instrument. Bob's plan was put on hold as other things took priority, and unfortunately, the guitar was stored away, unfinished, in an attic. Forty years passed with the instrument sitting and waiting until Bob rediscovered the guitar one day and decided it was time to finish it.

The hard work had been done years prior, and the only step left was adding the fretboard and strings. Guitars aren't the only thing Bob builds. There's a special place called The Oaks where he helps writers and dreamers who've met the Master Craftsman of the universe. People who need help shaping, sanding, and assembling the pieces of their instruments. There's a little chapel at The Oaks on top of a very steep hill. Inside, the chapel is carpeted and quiet, with lights that welcome you to a small stage. One afternoon Bob stood on the little stage and told the story of building his guitar. Bob's story was short in the telling but years in the making, and the message plucked a string deep inside me and the others in the room till it reverberated, and in some ways, it is still echoing.

I heard the creak of the guitar case as Bob opened the lid and grabbed the dark brown neck, lifting it with care. The fretboard was finished, and the new strings shone bright and brassy in the light. The guitar was finally ready to play. Bob extended his hands to a musician named Megan and asked if she would play a song.

The room was quiet as Bob explained that the guitar had never been played, but it became even quieter when Bob looked at Megan and said, "This guitar is yours now."

It had taken forty years to finish the guitar and no song had been played on it till this moment. All eyes locked on Megan as she lifted the strap over her head, and her hands found their place on the strings. I could see the rich brown tones of the wood and almost smell the oaky stain in the long, thin lines in the wood grain. Like a fine wine sitting in the cellar, this moment was magic, aged, and refined in its making. Under Megan's fingers, the strings, notes, and chords sang out powerfully, and not many of the eyes watching were dry as Megan reached the first chorus. The song was beautiful and sweet, and within the melody and meaning, I found a truth we all can use as we build our instruments.

The best dreams God places in our hearts are the ones that take years to make and moments to tell. It's the book that took years to write but only days to read, the homeless shelter that took years to build and an hour to open, and the diploma that took years to achieve and a moment to accept. The Master Craftsman helps with the assembly, sanding, shaping, and staining until we are ready to be fitted with the final piece to make our music in the world.

If you are in the assembly stage of your dreams, your strings are coming. If you have been through pain, challenges, and hardships, don't lose heart, your strings are coming. Perhaps you have spent more time in the attic than you planned. It's okay. Your song may be forty years in the making, but when God adds your strings, you will sing out a song rich with melody and meaning that reaches and reverberates deeply in the people around you.

As we wait for our dreams to be recognized and rediscovered in the attic, we often question God's timing. The attic can seem so far from the stage, but when the time is right, God will lead us to a place where our audience is waiting. He will open the case and hand you the dream he helped you craft. Don't be surprised if your time on the sawhorses has been less about repairing your physical cracks and more about reminding you who bought you. Our confidence in the water comes from knowing that no matter what we encounter, the One who bought us is the One who can keep us afloat. When we are anxious about our waiting times, it's our nature to rush the repairs, but our efforts usually result in extra holes in our hulls. Sometimes we cannot fix ourselves.

With God, it's your past that is sinking, not you. Your history may have holes, but your hull no longer will. We all have cracks we're working on, painting that needs doing, and we are all trying to get our oars working and to move forward. Jesus has the material for your patches and the paint for your scratches. He's repairing and preparing all of us for tomorrow and does all of this while we wait.

CHAPTER REFLECTION

No one likes to wait, but waiting doesn't have to be a waste. Much like the lesson we learned about failure in chapter 8, waiting presents an opportunity to grow. Instead of merely counting down the days until that thing you want to happen happens, ask God to help you learn from your waiting. Consider what he might be trying to teach you.

1. Think about a time when you waited on the sawhorses, a time you felt stuck or unable to make progress on something important. What did you learn in this time of waiting?
2. Does the correlation between bigger accomplishments and longer investments of time ring true in your life? Explain.
3. What strings are you waiting for God to add to your life? What might you learn or how might you grow as you wait?

Remember that Jesus has the material for your patches and the paint for your scratches. So don't waste seasons of waiting. Ask God what he is trying to teach you and how this season might make you more like Jesus.

CHAPTER 17

Made for Love

Standing at the back of the church in her white dress, she realized the walk down the aisle would not be long, but it would be lonelier than she expected. It was her wedding day, and the man she wanted to stand with at the end of the aisle was there, but the man she wanted by her side at the start of the aisle was not.

Many girls dream of walking down the aisle to marry their true love, and when they dream, they picture themselves walking down the aisle with their dad. This woman's dream was unfolding before her eyes. Her dress was beautiful, her hair perfect, and her makeup precisely the way she wanted. The minister is a longtime family friend, and the venue couldn't be better. The music was playing, the song she selected started, and the groom and groomsmen stood ready in their black tuxedos.

When she told her dad she was going to be married, his second question was about the song that was playing now.

"Are you sure he's the one?" he said. That was the first question.

She told him there would be no other man in her life like her dad but that this guy was very special and she loved him.

"Yes, he's the one, Dad," she said. When she said those words to her dad, she started crying.

Half happy tears, thinking about her wedding day, and half sad tears because this was a grown-up conversation, which meant she was grown up too. Her dad was also tearing up, so he asked a funny question. He always could ask something funny at the right time. He could take a tense situation and let the steam of stress out of it with one unexpected comment.

The second question was "What song will you walk down the aisle to?"

Though she had dreamed of it all her life, she hadn't put music to the moment in her mind, so the question caught her off guard.

"That's what you want to know?" she asked, wiping a tear from the corner of one eye with her finger.

"I think you should walk down the aisle to 'Hey, Hey, Good-bye.' Is that the name of that song?" he asked. He was waving one hand over his head like you would at a football game. The only thing missing was a giant foam finger.

"Dad!" she said. "I was thinking Pachelbel's Canon in D."

He pretended not to hear her as he was still singing, "Na na na na, na na na na, hey, hey, goodbye." He went on, "Then you could throw the bouquet and let out a 'Huh' on the beat."

"Yeah, that's what we're going to do," she said with a dramatic eye roll.

He loved it when she fired back at him in that tone.

He wondered if the guy she was marrying was ready for that tone.

"Not Canon in D," he said. "It's too traditional, and you have way too much soul to be traditional."

"Okay, what if I walk down the aisle to 'At Last' by Etta James?" she said.

"I like it." Her dad was smiling as he said it, but he was wiping a tear from his eye, and she could tell he also thought this felt like a grown-up conversation.

"At Last" was echoing through the church hall. She looked down at her bouquet and smiled. Maybe she should throw it early in his honor; he would have loved that.

The second lyric of the song stole her smile. Etta was singing about how her love had come along in the first lyric, and that was true; he was standing next to the minister. When Etta sang the second line about how her lonely days were over, that one made her cry. The first line felt right, but the second wasn't true, not now. She was marrying the man of her dreams, but she was walking with her arm wrapped around the elbow of a man she barely knew.

The arm that escorted her wasn't the one she had planned. A car accident changed their plans. She was grateful for the man standing beside her. She had her father to thank—this man was here because of him.

The night her father died, another man, a man who was dying, was given a second chance. Doctors transplanted the heart of this bride's father into the man who now stood arm in arm with her. This man wanted to be here. He wanted to bring the heart that had saved his life back to the family for whom the heart once beat.

They smiled at each other. It was awkward but sweet. The man, knowing he could never take the place of the one the bride wanted there, the bride feeling the void but glad to have even a part of her father there for her big day.

When they reached the end of the aisle, the minister asked, "Who gives this woman to be married today?"

The man took the bride's hand and held it to his chest. The heart beating there was one familiar to her. It beat the day she was born, the day she took her first steps, the day she graduated from high school, the day she first fell in love. It was beating still on this day.

"He does," the man said, his voice powered by the heart of the bride's father.

He barely got the words out. He was crying, she was crying, and the room wept for the man who was supposed to be there. The tears came and passed as the bride took her groom's hand, exchanged rings and vows, and they were married.

In our culture, we symbolize love with a heart, and I realize why when I think about this story of a bride and her father. A life without love is like a body missing a heart. Just as the heart powers the body, love powers the world. Just as the heart can outlast the body, love outlasts life. Love is the strongest force on our planet. God made us with love, out of love, to be loved, and to love. Love is a multiplied, exponential power that trumps every other aspect of creation.

We are all in need of a heart. If the bride's father had donated his money to the man who needed a heart, it wouldn't have helped. If he had donated his talent or time, it wouldn't have helped. Money, talent, and time can never supply what a man in need of a heart requires.

We are the same. God gives us talent, but he did not make us to exist on talent. God gives us time, and to some of us he entrusts money, but he did not make us to exist on either. God made us for love. Like a body needing its most vital organ, we require love to live.

Love connects us and sustains us. Love sets the expectation in relationships and then provides the means for living up to that expectation. Love tells our consciences what is right and wrong. Love is the answer to any argument, the solution to any barrier, and the best outcome for any dilemma. Our fiercest leaders proved the theory, from Martin Luther King, Jr., to Mother Teresa. Love is more powerful than any hate or wrongdoing, more potent than malice or slander. Nothing else could cause the Creator to descend to the dust and die. Love conquers division, crushes sin, and eliminates evil. The answer to living is love.

NAVIGATION SYSTEM

The plane I learned to fly in had a faded blue stripe down the side, a frayed brown seatbelt, and windows that rattled on takeoff. The Cessna 150 was so tiny our shoulders touched when my instructor and I wore our thick winter coats. Touching shoulders is strange because it's almost like cuddling. I liked my instructor, Chuck, but not in the cuddling kind of way, so at first, it was a bit awkward learning to fly. I logged many flight hours practicing takeoffs and landings while touching shoulders with Chuck, and soon I could fly the plane. Even better, I could land the plane, which is a big bonus for anyone wanting to return home. I remember how huge the cockpit became in that tiny plane when Chuck said, "It's time for you to solo." When my instructor got out, there was no one to be shoulder to shoulder with. I'd never been by myself in a plane with the engine running, and the plane sounded louder with only one person.

I remember peeling off the right earphone of my headset and shouting to Chuck, "Are you sure I'm ready?"

Chuck responded by laughing and closing the door. When you ask someone if you're ready and they respond by laughing, it makes you either very confident or very nervous. I was nervous.

I was on my own for the first time, and my hands shook as I gave the plane full throttle for my first solo takeoff. I climbed to three thousand feet and flew around the runway in the landing pattern. I turned onto the final approach, lowered the flaps for landing, and cut the throttle.

Landing a Cessna 150 is what Chuck liked to call "a controlled crash." It occurs by cutting the power to the engine and pointing the plane's nose toward the ground till at the last moment you pull back on the yoke, point the nose up, and let your wheels find the runway. Cutting the power to the engine on your first landing is an unnerving feeling. With the engine off, an eerie silence enveloped the pilot seat. I was nervous, but as I took a deep breath, I found something in the quiet of the cockpit. I found a voice. I had practiced these moments so many times with Chuck that I could hear his voice in my head repeating the things I needed to do to land the plane.

As I lined my plane up with the runway, a warning light flashed bright red over my forehead, and a loud horn sounded. The plane's stall warning was going off. If the plane's nose points too far up, it will lose its lift and fall from the sky. I could hear Chuck in my head saying, "Nose down and increase power."

God didn't intend for us to fly solo. God meant for us to do life shoulder to shoulder, helping each other find our way to new heights. From the beginning, God saw it wasn't good for Adam to be alone, so he created Eve, and God continues to place people around us to help us navigate all the nuances of our existence. No matter how alone you may feel, God has someone for you. Most of the time, he sends people to pilot with us, but we all have times when life's stall warning sounds its red-light alert. These are the moments when we feel as though our planes may fall from the sky: the death of a spouse, the loss of a child, and the emptiness in searching for our soulmate. During these times, the cockpit is quiet, the engine is off, and the seat where someone should sit shoulder to shoulder with you is empty. We are lost in these moments because we discover we are missing the one thing for which God made us. To love.

In a stall, Chuck would tell me to put the nose down and increase power. During life's stall moments, we must do the same. We put our nose down by bowing our heads in prayer. We add power by seeking our higher power.

If your airplane seems lonely and loud, perhaps it is because the person you were flying with is no longer there; nose down and add power. Perhaps the seat beside you is empty because you've yet to find the right person for your flight. It's okay— nose down and add power. Maybe you are in the middle of a divorce. Mid-flight, either your copilot bailed or you pushed them out. Either way, if you are currently in a stalled relationship, nose down and add power.

Feeling nervous about flying alone is normal. Take a breath and listen for the voice of the Master.

I listened to Chuck so much during my training that when I flew the Cessna 150 by myself, I could still hear him speaking in my head. The same is true for us. The more time we spend listening to the Master's voice, the more we will hear his voice over the noise of life's engine. It's the voice of the person who loves you more than anyone else ever will. It's the voice of one who knows you better than you know yourself. It's the voice of the One who made you, the voice of one who is constantly watching over you and wanting the best for you. Jesus died so you don't have to do life alone.

As we listen for the voice of the Master, we will discover the language he speaks is love.

Like the bride's father giving his heart to the man who walked his daughter down the aisle, our Father offers us his heart. He wants us to find his heartbeat in the chest of the people doing life beside us. The people walking beside us may not be the people we intended to share life's path with. We often don't get to choose who will be on our flight or who we will be seated by. It's okay. Don't leave your seat, and don't ask to be seated by an exit row. Buckle in and take a second look; the heart of the Father beats inside the people sitting in your row. When the bride's father donated his heart to a stranger, it started beating for someone else. The language of love calls us to donate our hearts to strangers. Line up your plane and land it; go all in with the people around you. Like it or not, we escort each other down the aisle toward our futures, arm in arm, in part two of God's greatest command to love each other. Jesus says the standard for how much we love others is how much we love ourselves.

CHAPTER REFLECTION

God made our hearts to be felt and heard. His greatest command is for us to love him more than anything and to love our neighbors as ourselves.[1] But did you catch the assumption in the second part of that command? You can't love your neighbor well if you don't love yourself.

1. Who are the people around you that God has placed in your life to love? How might loving yourself help you love them better?
2. Can you point to a time in your life when you focused on time, talent, or money more than you focused on love?
3. When was the last time you went "nose down" in prayer to connect with more power from our higher power?

How might doing so change your perspective? Your attitude?

Love is more powerful than any hate or wrongdoing, more potent than malice or slander. Do you believe this? Do you believe God made you for love? Ask God to help you see how much he loves you so that you might share his love with the people around you.

CHAPTER 18

Friend Power

Mike asked if I would be a pallbearer at his wife's funeral, and of course, I said yes. I was numb as I looked in the mirror, put on my black suit, and looped the tie around my neck. I was a groomsman at his wedding twenty-three years ago, and Mike said he wanted the men who stood beside him on his best day to stand with him on his worst.

He lost Heather unexpectedly, and just a few nights before, my phone had buzzed at 3:49 A.M. with a text from Mike.

I called him as soon as I read what he had written, and we cried together as he told me how she had died. I'm sure the heavy emptiness in my chest was nothing compared to his, but I was still left short of breath and with no words to say. I wish I had something with which to comfort my friend or some way to spare him the pain, but all I could do was be there with him in the moment.

When tragedies come and our presence is all we have to offer, we feel inadequate.

We want to be people who bring answers to pain, but sometimes that power is beyond us. We wish we were magic-wand wavers who could conjure a spell of instant healing. The truth is we are ointment and salve applied gently over time to take out the sting and let the wound heal on its own.

We all need 3:00 A.M. friends. People we can call, no matter how late or early, especially when we need them most. We need people who stand beside us on our best days and our worst because it's the standing-beside part that's often worth more than any words we offer.

God was the first to say it isn't good for us to be alone. God wired us with both a need for companions and the need to be companions. Friendships are essential for happiness because God made us this way. Jesus surrounded himself with a group of people he counted on and cared for, and we should do the same.

RIDING SHOTGUN

In the 1800s, Wells Fargo started a stagecoach service to carry passengers from Missouri to San Francisco. It was a dangerous twenty-eight-hundred-mile trip, often with robbers waiting to steal whatever the stagecoach and its passengers carried. For the safety of the passengers, the company issued shotguns to the stagecoach drivers and guards.

The guard sitting next to the person steering the stagecoach became known as the shotgun messenger, and his primary job was protecting the driver. Carrying the shotgun was less about being a good shot and more about having the courage to stay with the driver no matter how rough the trip became.

Bravery, grit, and loyalty were prerequisites for the position, which meant only the toughest cowboys, like Wyatt Earp, were suited. When Wyatt Earp first came to Tombstone, Arizona, before becoming the famous U.S. marshal at the O.K.

Corral, his first job was as a shotgun messenger. Tales of tough cowboys brought nostalgia to the shotgun messenger position, and it became known as "riding shotgun."[1]

God knew from the start we need sidekicks who shout "Shotgun," friends who buckle in beside us for the long haul. Friends more concerned about the driver than the destination.

Peter was one of Jesus' closest friends, but he wasn't the most courageous when roosters crowed, and he's famous for lacking the faith necessary to walk on water. Still, Peter stayed close to Jesus, close enough to reach for his sword when the mob came to arrest Jesus in Gethsemane. As good friends, we aren't always perfect when standing beside each other in tragic situations. We don't always know what to say, but riding shotgun isn't about being a good shot with our words or actions; it's about buckling in beside our friends for the tough times.

We need to buckle in beside the people in our lives who need us.

Buckle in beside the friend who has lost their job.

Buckle in beside the friend who is going through a divorce.

Buckle in beside the friend who has lost someone they love.

POKER BUDDIES

When the wilderness calls, manly men don't take messages. My five friends and I heard the call on a primal level and dusted off our survival skills. We heard nature's summons, and we went into the woods to answer. We drove fifty-one miles, not twenty, not thirty, fifty-one miles out of town. We took the road slightly smaller than the main highway and kept driving even after passing the omelet shop at the end of town.

Living on the edge, we left at night, past sunset, driving at the witching hour of 7:30 P.M.

We were roughing it, so we packed everything we usually have at our houses, only in travel sizes.

Why risk it all to taste freedom? Because our wives had given us permission to taste freedom. When your wife grants permission for freedom, you grab on to it with both hands and you don't let go until the designated time to return home.

We made a wilderness pact on our drive as we sipped special-order lattes. Any meat we ate had to be meat we had killed. Once we realized someone had already killed the animal in the bag of beef jerky, we made a new pact. Anyone who opened a new pack of beef jerky had to use their teeth like a man. I recently had dental work done, so we decided it was okay if I started tearing open the beef jerky with my fingers and then finished dramatically with my teeth and a growl.

We made the conscious choice to live off what the land provided.

In this case, the cabin we rented in the woods provided dishes and beds. We congratulated ourselves for not sleeping in cozy beds like a bunch of Girl Scouts selling cookies. We were in the wild, which meant sleeping in cabin beds that were slightly less cozy than our beds at home.

Were we roughing it? We were in a location where cellphones didn't have five bars of service, only two, so yes, I would call that roughing it.

We drank in the desolation of the cabin, realizing there was only one TV and basic cable.

Really basic cable.

We had learned survival skills from shows like *Alone* and Bear Grylls's *Man vs. Wild,* but out here, we were on our own because those shows were unavailable on basic cable.

We unpacked and started a fire in the potbelly stove using the manly one-click lighter (the long kind, so we didn't burn our manly fingers).

We sat around the only table in the cabin and wondered, *Now what?*

We looked around the table at each other's faces.

No sports, Starbucks, or Facebook because manly men in cabins make verbal commitments to limit their screen time.

It was awkward at first, but then we remembered we were men. When real men gather for a game around a table, they play only one game.

Poker.

Real men in cabins in the wild wilderness play poker.

I ripped the beef jerky bag open with my teeth and yelled, "Deal 'em up!"

We searched our suitcases for cards but found none. We considered driving into town to buy a pack of cards, but it was fifty-one miles, not twenty, not thirty, fifty-one miles back to town.

I saw discouragement on the faces of the men around me. I saw defeat in their eyes, but then I remembered there might be a deck of cards in my car. I went to the car and searched beneath the dim overhead light. With my detective skills heightened and focused, I looked everywhere in plain sight. They were not on the dashboard or the front seat. (God help me, why was this so hard?)

I started to do what I usually do in this situation and call my wife to ask her where the cards were, but I stopped myself.

If ever there was a time for me to prove I was a man, this was it. I put my hand under the driver's seat. "Ew, yogurt." *How old was that?* As I looked under the seat, I found a bottle of formula so old the plastic was swollen and bulging. As I picked it up, air leaked out and I gagged at the smell of what was now homemade cottage cheese.

A lesser man would have turned back, but that night in the wilderness, I was not a lesser man. I put my hand under the passenger seat and felt around blindly.

An instant adrenaline rush—the cards were there!

I pulled them out and held them up to the dim light in the car. A flood of trepidation washed over me because I had forgotten what kind of cards these were. Was I really about to introduce this element to this group of guys?

I had no other option; this was the only choice.

Desperate times call for desperate measures, so I manned up.

I brought in the deck and slammed it on the table confidently.

Laughter erupted as every man beheld the pink deck of Disney Princess cards.

You don't know fear until you sit across from a man and all you're holding is a pair of Princess Jasmines, and you're sure the man next to you has three Snow Whites and two Pocahontases (a full house of princesses!).

We were men in the woods, brave and fierce with knuckles full of pink Disney Princess cards, and we laughed so hard there were tears.

It didn't matter what kind of cards we had; it didn't matter what game we played. Sometimes the deck isn't just stacked against you—it's completely missing and you have to find your own cards, but I've found such moments are the most memorable parts of this journey.

You never worry if you're good enough when you have friends like that group of guys. You never wonder if you fit in—because you know you do. Looking around the poker table, I realized I had a full house, not in the cards I was holding, but in the friends sitting with me. I also realized the friends around the table took a while to assemble. There were older friendships seated there and newer friendships too. Sometimes the cards life deals aren't the ones we need, and we have to trade in a few for a better hand. Who's sitting around your poker table? Are they people on whom you can count? If not, maybe it's time for new cards. Life is too much of a gamble to wonder if we have the right friends. If the friends you have aren't the kind that will go all in with you, raise the stakes.

PEOPLE ON THE PLATFORM

In Perth, Australia, a man was boarding a commuter train when his foot slipped into the gap between the train and the platform. The man fell as far as one leg would let him until he was wedged between the train and the platform. He tried to free himself but was unable. A quick-thinking conductor came up with a solution. The conductor ordered everyone off the train and, on the count of three, had them all push against the side of the train. The crowd, collectively pushing against the side of the train, rocked the train just enough to free the man's leg.[2]

We need people in our lives who will step off the train and help us get out of the places where we get stuck. We need people who will push against our problems, people who will lean in to our lives, and conductors committed to helping us get out of the gaps life throws at us. We don't possess enough power to move the big trains, but a group of friends working together does.

God never intended us to do life alone; our design doesn't support a solo existence, but sometimes being in relationships with the wrong people is worse than being alone. We need people we can count on who will be there for us.

Jesus' closest friends dropped everything when he asked them to. Peter, Andrew, James, and John left homes, jobs, and families without knowing where they were going. We typically don't ask people to leave their homes to be our friends, but if it came down to it, a few of the guys sitting around my poker table would at least consider it. We all have times when we must take a second look at the characters sitting around our tables and ask ourselves if they are the kind of friends we can call at 3:00 A.M.

We're all destined for loss at some point; we need friends who will stand with us on our best and worst days. We need friends who are the comfort that words can never bring.

Who is sitting around your poker table?

We need 3:00 A.M. friends, friends who shout "Shotgun" and buckle in beside you when needed. We need to surround ourselves with friends committed to riding with us even when the wheels come off, friends who buckle into the passenger seat beside us, more concerned about the driver than the destination.

CHAPTER REFLECTION

God never intended us to live alone. We all have a deep need in our hearts for connection—to know people and be known by them. While it is good to have friends who are not Christians (friendship is often an important prerequisite to sharing our faith), it is important to have friends who love Jesus and point you to him. If you don't have friends who pray for you and encourage you to follow Jesus, it might be time to reconsider the friends seated around your poker table.

1. Who in your life prays for you or encourages you in your faith? What is one step you could take this week to develop a friendship centered on Jesus?
2. Do you have friends you encourage and pray for regularly? What is one small way you could encourage or support one of your friends this week?
3. What keeps us from cultivating more meaningful friendships? How can you develop more meaningful relationships with friends you already have?

You need friends who will stand with you on your best and worst days. Having those kinds of friends, however, requires striving to be that kind of friend to others. Ask God to help you see the value of the friends he has placed in your life. Ask him also to help you be a more faithful, supportive friend to the people closest to you.

CHAPTER 19

Broadcast Station

People don't plan to take a two-year-old to the opera unless the babysitter backs out at the last minute. People don't take a two-year-old to the opera unless their boss is selected as a soprano and is singing in the show. People don't take a two-year-old to the opera if there are any other options. People don't take a two-year-old to the opera.

My boss bought the tickets, so we decided it was better to take our two-year-old with us rather than I go to the concert solo. We brought my daughter, Casey, with us knowing she would have to sit on our laps, knowing it was a three-hour concert. What were we thinking? We picked up our tickets and discovered our seats were in the center section's middle row. Of course they were. The seats were so close together our knees touched the seats in front of us. We were already getting dirty looks because Casey dropped a toy on the ground and it rolled under the seat in front of us.

"We shouldn't have done this," I said to my wife.

"Let's take her out to the lobby," my wife said.

Before we could act, the lights dimmed, the orchestra went

silent, and the crowd applauded as the master of ceremonies stepped onto the stage. To get up now or during the show would disturb an entire row, maybe an entire section, possibly an entire theater. So I sat there, my tension building with the music, realizing we had three hours to go.

The lady sitting next to the child on my lap had no kind greeting. No "What a cutie" or "You're brave to bring her here." Not even a "Hey stupid, this is an opera, and she is a toddler; what were you thinking?" Instead, I saw her give her date an elbow as she pointed at me and my daughter with a tilt of her head.

Then I smelled it.

Yep, Casey's diaper needed to be changed, and I'm pretty sure the lady beside me knew it too.

Ever feel like the curtain is going up and you didn't plan well enough? Ever feel like everyone is watching and no one is rooting for you? Ever try to keep a baby calm when you aren't? We sat in that situation, there in the center section in the middle row.

Two songs in, Casey said the one two-syllable word all parents of toddlers know to be a serious warning.

"Hung-gee," Casey said.

Hung-gee is the toddler word for *hungry*, and as many parents will attest, a hung-gee toddler is a ticking time bomb problem. Hungry toddlers are short-tempered creatures who, if not fed soon, will explode in loud tantrums. Tantrums that have no place in an opera.

Houston, we have a problem. We are in the center section, middle row of an opera, and we have a "hung-gee." I could hear the timpani playing in the orchestra, but the pounding pulse in my head was way louder.

With my focus on Casey, I wasn't paying much attention to the opera, but it turns out Casey was. The orchestra played and the sold-out crowd listened. The sopranos sang and the production crescendoed. The song swelled, the choir crested, and there was a break. A moment of silence when the flutes froze, the piano paused, and the singers stopped. It wasn't the end of the piece, just a dramatic rest, and it was precisely in this quiet that Casey decided to make her opera debut.

I read the playbill and Casey's name wasn't listed, but that didn't stop her from playing a lead role. Standing on my lap, she held both hands over her head and sang out a single loud opera note.

Oh, but that was just the warm-up.

Luckily only I heard the trumpet section blaring out from inside her diaper, but everyone heard her commentary when Casey, in her tiny toddler voice, said, "Oopsie."

I wanted to crawl under my seat.

The entire room remained silent. The opera interrupted, my embarrassment was on full display.

I reached up to cover Casey's mouth to stop other sounds or words, but it was too late. Casey stole the show as every eye turned away from the stage and looked instead to the middle section, center row, and the "hung-gee" opera toddler.

God created each of us with a voice, and there will come a time in life's opera when you will have a chance to sing out. If you think you aren't talented enough to share your story, remember even a single note can steal the show, and all of us have at least one good note inside.

CO-MOON-YUN

In 1969 two astronauts, Neil Armstrong and Buzz Aldrin, landed a spacecraft on the moon. The long trip from Cape Canaveral on earth to the Sea of Tranquility on the moon was full of stressful moments, so before Neil and Buzz took the first steps on the surface of the moon, NASA decided they needed rest. During this interlude, Buzz Aldrin took communion or, as I like to call it, co-moon-yun. The first food eaten on the moon was communion bread, and the first liquid consumed on the moon's surface was communion wine. Buzz Aldrin was an elder at Webster Presbyterian Church and a strong man of faith, so he decided from his seat in the lunar lander to turn on the microphone and broadcast communion. Humans had never spoken to God from the moon before, but that day Buzz broadcast his words and spoke not just to the created on earth but also to the Creator in the heavens from the heavens. Buzz broke the silence by saying, "I would like to invite each person listening in, wherever and whomever he may be, to contemplate for a moment the events of the past few hours and to give thanks in his own individual way."[1] Aldrin ate the bread, and the wine in lunar gravity floated and curled up the side of the cup as he drank it.

That day one man took communion, but he did so in a way, in a place, at a time, that would shine out to all of the people of earth. An estimated 650 million people watched the Apollo 11 moon landing, roughly one-fifth of the world's population at the time.[2] Housewives stopped hanging out laundry, businessmen left meetings, and school classrooms paused. In the opera of the earth, one-fifth of the world's population stopped for a moment, and in that moment a man had communion on the moon.

The sun's light reflected off the moon, and the Son's light shone from the moon's surface to the world below as an astronaut paused quietly in his capsule to see the Savior.

We may never sit in a silent lunar lander waiting to broadcast to a fifth of the world's population, but there is an audience for you. For some of us, our audiences are arenas full of people who need to hear our voices. For others, our audience is a Bible class, youth conference, or the congregation who has paused to listen to our preaching from the pulpit. For others, it's an audience of one that needs the message only we can deliver.

It's the friend who lost his wife tragically and needs a phone call from you. It's the neighbor whose husband is not kind and who needs your single broadcast of encouragement. The child always picked last, needing you to talk to them first. It's the person who feels lonely in a crowded room, needing you to pull up a chair and chat. It's the woman who survived a similar trauma, the one you can speak about because it's the one from which you've healed.

Your time at the microphone may come after you've raised your children and find yourself surrounded by an audience of new parents. After you've stopped drinking and stayed sober, it may be time to speak to others who are trying to put down the bottle. We aren't all professional broadcasters, and very few are professional opera singers, but each of us has an audience.

BROADCAST STATION

It's 2:51 A.M. as I'm writing this chapter. After I finished writing the second chapter of this book, I started having trouble sleeping. At first I thought my insomnia was just restless tossing in bed as the lightbulb in my brain attracted thought moths to it.

I was nervous the moths would leave and the ideas would be lost if I slept, so I stayed awake.

By chapter 6, I was getting out of bed at midnight and following the thought moths down the hall to my office. I'd sit in the red recliner in the corner and use my MacBook to pen moths to paper for an hour before returning to bargain with the bed for sleep. As the pages stacked up, the gaps in my sleep grew, the bags under my eyes sagged, and the time in the red recliner increased.

Looking inward, I discovered a broadcast station inside me that had previously been silent. A small soundproof booth with blue foam-padded walls and a red light labeled "on air" was waiting each night to send out the message I wanted to share with others.

In a series of midnight writing sessions, I plotted out chapters on two giant marker boards in my office. I arranged my thoughts in the order I wanted them to appear in each chapter. After many months of organizing, rearranging, and thinking, I finally had everything I wanted to include in the book represented on marker boards.

My book was finished; it just wasn't written yet.

Your book is finished, too, but you have to write it. God installed every piece of equipment needed for writing when he created humankind in the Garden of Eden.

There's a broadcast station inside each of us, and we each have an opportunity to reach an audience with the message we send over its airwaves. Any DJ will tell you the time to talk is when the on-air light is lit. God illuminates the on-air light in all of us at some point. For some, the microphone is a pulpit; others rely on a keyboard or the pen. Still others speak best with actions. Whatever kind of radio waves you send out on your broadcast station, lean in to the microphone and be heard. Send out your broadcast megawatt strong with the volume knob turned up all the way.

Figure out the things that stand between you and your audience and get rid of them. Buy the Post-it notes, hang the marker boards, and skip the sleep (for a time) if that's what it takes to get your message out.

We all have stories to write, but we are all in different stages of writing. You may have a beginning to your story that will help me as I'm finding the ending to mine. We are all adding sweet, tragic, funny, and profoundly moving parts to the chapters we are living and writing, and sharing is a great benefit to both the writer and the reader.

Much of my career has been spent helping people recognize the brilliant parts of their stories because, as the authors of our lives, we're caught up in the characters and the dialogue and often miss our most monumental chapters. In our lives' opera, we are often nervous about sharing our voices. We fear the timing may not be right, but when the message you were born to broadcast is laid on your heart, it will wake you from your sleep of silence. I don't know if your audience is small, medium, or large, but I do know someone in the world needs your broadcast. Step up to the microphone, clear your throat, and be heard. Broadcast your experience, love, kindness, courage, and empathy. No matter what format you use, be it written word, spoken word, by example, music, or poetry, I'm convinced that as you find your frequency, you will also find value in yourself.

CHAPTER REFLECTION

Who is your audience? No matter if it's an audience of one or one hundred thousand, someone will benefit from you sharing your story with the world. When we are clear about who our audiences are, we can be intentional about how we share Jesus with them.

1. Make a list of the people in your audience—the people in your life you can encourage, bless, or influence.

2. Honestly assess the message you are broadcasting to your audience. How might your message need to change to more faithfully point people around you to Jesus?

3. What are ways you can broadcast God's love to others? How might God use your unique gifts or situation to point others to Jesus?

What are you broadcasting? Whether you know it or not, you are sending out a message to the world. Our broadcast light is always on because we are always sending out something. Double-check that the message you send out is positive and reflects the blessings you've been given.

EPILOGUE

When people say things are bigger in Texas, that includes things you would never want to exist in your house. I lived in Texas for a time, and I remember all too clearly one night when I was sitting in our living room in Dallas and saw something run across the floor and behind the TV stand. I was on the phone with my wife, and I said, "I think I just saw a mouse run behind the TV."

Out of town, Maggie was immediately disgusted at the idea of coming home to a varmint, no matter what kind it was, roaming free in the house.

"Can you get it?" she said.

Standing up and switching my phone to the other ear, I walked to the side of the TV and leaned down for a better look.

"Oh!" is what I think I said.

"What's wrong?" Maggie said.

"It's not a mouse." I had never seen one this big and was nervous, wondering if it was poisonous.

"What's wrong? Did you get it?"

Maggie was bothered because I wasn't giving a good report

on the situation, but I didn't know how to answer her. The creature I was looking at had starred in Maggie's worst nightmares and phobias.

Maggie's voice was louder in my ear. "Tell me what it is."

"I think it's a tarantula," I said. I slid the edge of the TV stand back a little and got a clearer view. I'm not sure if it was my subconscious, but I took a step back, and it was a step toward the front door. I noticed the phone was slippery in my hand from sweat.

"A what!" Maggie said. "Are you serious?"

I was. I said, "If it's not a tarantula, it looks like one, and I've never seen a spider as big as this one."

"Step on it!"

I couldn't. I imagined it mashing down like a giant tomato under my shoe or flipping over at the last minute and latching on to the sole of my Nike. Nope.

I said, "Not stepping on it, ever!"

"Can you catch it?"

I thought for a second, then answered. "Can you fly home tonight and catch it yourself?"

I was half joking. I grabbed a Pringles can off the kitchen counter, peeled back the transparent lid, and dumped out the chips. Flipping the can upside down, I moved into position to lower the opening of the can over the spider. I couldn't tell what Maggie said as I set the phone down, but I was sure she was still asking questions.

"Slowly," I whispered to myself. "Easy now."

As I got closer, I began to realize the Pringles can wasn't big enough. The spider's body would fit in the can, but the legs were not going to fit. I'm not typically afraid of spiders, but I was now scared of this one.

There's a famous line from the movie *Jaws* when one of the men chasing the giant shark says, "You're going to need a bigger boat."[1] I said that line under my breath to myself, and when I did, I briefly stopped lowering the Pringles can.

Things happened quickly after that. The spider twitched, and I reacted, lowering the can fast and furious. I was right in my estimation. The spider's body did fit into the can and the legs did not. In cookie-cutter fashion the can snapped off all eight legs, which now lay moving by themselves on the floor.

I've found that the things we don't love about ourselves are a lot like giant Texas spiders. If left to roam free, they eventually find a way to sink our self-esteem and freeze us with fear.

I hope this book is like a giant Pringles can, one big enough to cripple the spiders creeping in the corners of your confidence.

Loving ourselves is a big topic, maybe the biggest. Jesus tells us the greatest command is to love God and our neighbor, and the standard he gives us for loving our neighbor is how much we love ourselves. It's a topic we all need help with, so I enlisted the help of two incredible coaches in my attempt to tackle it. My friends and coaches, Kim and Bob, both knew when to cheer from the sidelines and when to blow the whistle, step onto the field, and give direction. During the writing of chapter 3, Bob blew his whistle.

Bob told me to keep each chapter under twenty-five hundred words. Our conversation went something like this:

He asked, "Do you know why you want to keep each chapter under twenty-five hundred words, Bryan?"

"No, I don't."

"Because that's how many words most people can read before their legs fall asleep."

"Why do people's legs fall asleep while reading?"

"Because statistically, most people do the bulk of their reading on the toilet," Bob said while laughing.

Bob and Kim both provided much more than just advice on

the length of each chapter. Kim's coaching had fewer toilet references, but I'm deeply thankful for both Bob and Kim and the wise counsel they provided. I wish I had bigger or better words to describe how grateful I am to Bob and Kim for their profound influence and endless inspiration. None of us would run nearly as far or as fast without the cheering of great people from the sidelines, but we also need people in our lives who are willing to blow the whistle and step onto the field.

I pray this book was an encouraging cheer from the sidelines and hope you've heard the coach's whistle in these words. I hope you have discovered in me another person willing to step onto the field with you.

I should point out that the hospice stories from my experience working as a chaplain in southeast Ohio are real. Most of them are stories about a single person and some are a composite of different people I was privileged to meet and work with in their final days. All the names were changed to protect each family's privacy and as respect for the people who have passed away.

To write of our internal design is to tell our stories, so I've interwoven tales of my daughter, my wife, my friends, my family, and my childhood because each of these comprises the air in the bellows of the instrument that makes the music in my world; and the same is true for you.

As for my story, my children's book *Stripey Bottom* is still for sale on Amazon, and as far as I know, it is still banned at the Christian school my daughter used to attend. *Stripey Bottom* was banned for two bad words. Which bad words? I guess you'll just have to buy the book to find out.

I haven't made a third attempt to reach the top of Half Dome yet, but if you're reading this, it means my grizzly-sized dream to write a book, the one birthed the day after failing to reach the top of Half Dome, has come true.

As for my time spent battling hornets in college, eventually we found a vacuum bag and placed it in the vacuum. At last the hornets ended up where we had planned, proving cartoon logic can work in everyday life.

We haven't played poker in a while, but I'm still riding shotgun with my friends Matt, Mike, Tom, and Stephen, who make up the Christian band Lost-n-Found. We've crossed the United States more than a few times, mostly in vehicles likely to break down. If you'd like to hear some great music, you can find our songs on Apple Music and the group's Facebook page at Lost-n-Found, www.facebook.com/lost.n.found.acappella.

News of the Pringles-can spider spread to my sister in California, the only person as grossed out by spiders as much as my wife. As I told Stacia the story over the phone, she was disgusted at the thought of such a beast running loose in our house. She was so disgusted I realized I had a golden opportunity. Remember, this is the person I convinced to lick the electric racetrack and took with me on typhoon roller-skate rides.

"You have to see the size of this thing," I said to Stacia.

"You still have it?" she asked.

"I do. I kept it because it's *Guinness World Records* stuff."

"Ewwww, I don't ever want to see that."

"I know you're saying that, but you really need to see this; I wish there were some way for you to see it in person."

The conversation ended, but I'm sure Stacia thought about our phone call a few times that night. She probably double-checked under her bed and made sure nothing crept into her covers. She thought about it—I was sure of it. As I said, I realized I had a golden opportunity, so I sent an empty Pringles can to her in the mail the next day. I wish I could have seen her face when she opened the package. My brother-in-law, Michael, said that when she saw the Pringles can, all she said was, "Oh no, he didn't."

The boat I bought at auction, the one Casey sanded a hole through, is finally in the water. I discovered I was lousy at rowing on the maiden voyage and almost capsized it more than once, but I'm getting better and there's a lesson to learn in every attempt.

Maggie is still running. She hasn't run into any more bears, save one we saw on the hike down from Half Dome. Maggie was part of our group who hiked Half Dome, and she made it farther than I did. I consider any run or hike—figurative or literal—when I keep up with her to be a success.

Forrest Fenn's treasure was found while I was writing this book. A man named Jack Stuef figured out the clues and found the treasure chest buried in Wyoming.

Like the big Nashville organ, as you peer through the window into your inner workings, you're going to find a treasure more valuable than anything Forrest Fenn buried. You're going to find a love God intended you to have not just for others but for yourself. As you do, you may find God has tuned your broadcast station to an audience who wants to hear your story. I know I would. Drop me an email at bryan@bryancrum .com. I'd love to hear from you.

You may not realize it, but you and I became part of something together when you bought this book. We are helping orphans. Together we are changing their stories. We are bringing them food, clean water, and clothes. We are providing education, safety, and support because all the proceeds from the sale of this book are being given to a nonprofit organization called Boomerang Ministry Corp (www.boomerangministrycorp.com). Boomerang is on a mission to help these children, and since you have purchased this book, you are helping them too.

I have one final thought to leave you with. There's a rosebush planted in the flower bed outside my house. This plant is from a cutting from the rosebush planted outside the house I grew up in. When Maggie and I were dating, I picked roses from the original bush to give to Maggie, and so my mom gave us a cutting from it as a wedding gift. When I come home from work, the rosebush greets me. Some days, as I step out of my car, I pick a rose if one is in bloom, and I carry it inside to Maggie.

I think God places roses as reminders in our lives. They go unnoticed at times, but they are there for our benefit if we will only stop and admire them. One night, I was reading about Halley's Comet and how it wouldn't appear again until the year 2061. I counted up how old I would be when it reappeared. I realized I wanted to be with Maggie when the comet passed overhead again, and for some reason, I thought of the rosebush planted outside of our house all these years, and I wondered if it would be around then too. I wrote a poem for Maggie that I've included as the closing of this book. I'm including it because it's been one way God has reminded me of the valuable things and people he's planted in my life and because I hope in some way this book has been a "reminding rose" in your life. I've written these pages just for you, hoping they will remind you of the great value God has placed inside of you.

I'm grateful this book will assist Boomerang Ministry Corp in its work, but I wrote this book and all its stories in hopes it will help you as you write your story. You have pages to fill and great, thrilling chapters to live. God wants you to live powerfully with an awareness of the incredible talent and quality he has embedded inside you. At the end of your story the One who is bright is waiting on the other side of a very thin curtain. He died to save you, he loves you more than anyone else, and he can't wait to welcome you.

I hope your legs haven't fallen asleep in the process of reading these chapters, and I hope this book has reminded you of how valuable and loved you are. Most, my dear neighbor, I hope this book has helped you love yourself more.

POEM FOR MAGGIE

"Halley and the Rosebush"

THE COMET

*She came before city lights and passed through black skies
   above the earth with an understanding that my name
   and yours would be written together*
*She came again before photographs could capture her
   light, her arc a knowing grin of our destiny*
*She came again before my birth, passing and aware you
   would find me and I would love you*
*She came again smiling down on me, a boy in a snowy
   desert, smiling because your future and mine would
   soon be side by side*

THE ROSEBUSH

*It slept in the earth only a seed the year before we had
   found one another*
It was born and budded in its first spring when I loved you

It bloomed, and I loved you still
It grew and was picked by me to share with you again and
    again and again
It was planted anew to the sound of crickets announcing
    our home in 1998

The comet keeps coming back every 75 years, hoping to
    catch a glimpse of us
She's jealous of the rosebush who sees us every spring

In 1758, she missed us
In 1835, she wanted so badly to see us
In 1910, she was a little too soon in her timing
in 1986, she saw me but not you

This time she will see us both
I will be 88 and you 87, and Halley will finally see what
    she's been looking for all this time

It's planned
The perfect night, the perfect date
A coffee
A walk
A dance
A look up into the sky
I'll drop to a creaky old knee
There under the sky of that night, Halley will pass over us
    and smile down with her starry eyes as I hand you a
    rose from that same rosebush
The year will be 2061, and I will be in love with you

ACKNOWLEDGMENTS

Neighbor, Love Yourself, like any published book, was a team effort, and I've been blessed with incredible teammates. Thank you, Bob Goff and Kimberly Stuart. Bob's cheers from the sidelines were terrific, but his ability to help me see the writer inside myself was life-changing. I continue to be in awe of Kim's ninja-like writing skills and her talent for delivering powerful gut-check critiques in a positive and motivating way. Jamie Chavez completed a firm first round of edits that helped shape this book, and Drew Dixon provided much reassurance and masterful final edits. Dan Balow of the Steve Laube Agency was instrumental in connecting this book with Water-Brook at Penguin Random House; chances are you would not be reading these words without Dan's vital work. Countless friends took the time to read various chapters of the manuscript and offer advice: Kathy Swatzel, Kerrie Gabler, Dawn Fitzpatrick, and Jill Vickerts. Katie Nguyen and FrontGate Media helped broadcast quotes from the book out into the social media world long before this book was a book. The wonderful WaterBrook and Penguin Random House team saw a message within the manuscript and heard a heart that longed to be shared. Praying over these pages with these people was powerful!

I hope I haven't forgotten anyone.

Special thanks to Maggie and Casey Crum, who read more of my words than anyone else and told me to keep writing.

NOTES

INTRODUCTION: We Aren't Missing Any Parts

1. Nick Kurczewski, "Lamborghini Supercars Exist Because of a 10-Lira Tractor Clutch," *Car and Driver*, November 16, 2018, www.caranddriver.com/features/a25169632/lamborghini-supercars-exist-because-of-a-tractor.
2. "The Argument Between Lamborghini and Ferrari," Motor Web Museum, www.motorwebmuseum.it/en/places/cento/the-argument-between-lamborghini-and-ferrari.
3. R. J. Bachman, "Behind the Lamborghini Ferrari Feud," Attic Capital, July 31, 2023, https://atticcapital.com/behind-the-lamborghini-ferrari-feud.

CHAPTER 1: Unearthing Our Inner Worth

1. Sarah Kuta, "You Can Own a Piece of Forrest Fenn's Treasure," *Smithsonian Magazine*, November 28, 2022, www.smithsonian-mag.com/smart-news/forrest-fenn-treasure-auction-180981183.
2. "The Hunt for Forrest Fenn's Treasure," *CBS News*, December 22, 2021, www.cbsnews.com/pictures/forrest-fenn-treasure-hunt.
3. Clayton Sandell, Michell Kessel, and Connor Burton, "People Continue to Seek Reported Hidden Treasure in the Rocky Mountains, Despite Fatal Attempts," *ABC News*, January 12,

2018, https://abcnews.go.com/US/people-continue-seek-reported-hidden-treasure-rocky-mountains/story?id=51766060.

CHAPTER 2: Recognizing Divine Sophistication

1. Exodus 4:2, NIV.
2. Exodus 4:2, NIV.

CHAPTER 3: Good Words

1. Matt Houston and Mykal Vincent, "Fire Destroys House, Stops at Scriptures Written on Studs," WAFB, February 3, 2020, www.wafb.com/2020/02/03/fire-destroys-house-stops-scriptures-written-studs.
2. "Massive Fire at Louisiana Home Stops at Scripture Verses Written on Studs," 5News, February 3, 2020, www.5newsonline.com/article/news/massive-fire-at-louisiana-home-stops-at-scripture-verses-written-on-studs/527-cd919d9c-b665-41f4-99c2-87dcf36b4efa.
3. Genesis 1:31, NIV.

CHAPTER 4: Bad Words

1. "What Is Active Dying?" Crossroads Hospice & Palliative Care, www.crossroadshospice.com/hospice-resources/end-of-life-signs/what-is-active-dying.
2. Proverbs 18:21.

CHAPTER 5: Purpose Power

1. Myles Munroe, *In Charge: Finding the Leader Within You* (New York: FaithWords, 2008).
2. 2 Timothy 1:7.
3. Isaiah 41:10.
4. James 1:6, NIV.

CHAPTER 6: The Power to Picture Our Future

1. Hebrews 12:1–3, NIV.

CHAPTER 7: The Power to Paint Our Present

1. "Vincent van Gogh, *The Starry Night,* Saint Rémy, June 1889," MoMA Learning, www.moma.org/learn/moma_learning/vincent-van-gogh-the-starry-night-1889.
2. Mark 11:23, NIV.
3. 1 Samuel 17:46, NIV.

CHAPTER 9: Castle of Confidence

1. "The Historic Loveland Castle and Museum," Loveland Castle, https://lovelandcastle.com.
2. Timothy S. Miller, "Moments in the History of Medievalism: Historic Loveland Castle," *The Fish in Prison* (blog), www.the-fishinprison.com/blog/moments-in-the-history-of-medievalism-historic-loveland-castle.
3. Alexandra Charitan, "Modern Knights in Southern Ohio: Inside Loveland Castle, One Man's Medieval Masterpiece," Roadtrippers, https://roadtrippers.com/magazine/loveland-castle-ohio.
4. 2 Corinthians 4:8–10, NIV.
5. William Shakespeare, *The Merchant of Venice,* ed. Barbara A. Mowat and Paul Werstine (New York: Simon & Schuster Paperbacks, 2009), act III, scene 1, lines 46–55.

CHAPTER 12: Our Flashlight Feature

1. James 1:16–17.
2. Romans 6:1–3.

CHAPTER 13: Our Check-Engine Light

1. Anne Geddes, www.annegeddes.com.
2. Genesis 3:2, 6.
3. Romans 7:19.

CHAPTER 14: Our Lifesaving Component

1. John 8:1–11.

CHAPTER 16: Sawhorses

1. Isaiah 40:31.
2. Isaiah 40:31.

CHAPTER 17: Made for Love

1. Matthew 22:36–40.

CHAPTER 18: Friend Power

1. Wikipedia, "Riding Shotgun," last modified August 1, 2023, https://en.wikipedia.org/wiki/Riding_shotgun.
2. "Man Trapped by Train 'Amazed' by Commuters Who Saved His Leg," ABC News, August 7, 2014, https://abcnews.go.com/International/man-trapped-train-amazed-commuters-saved-leg/story?id=24882972.

CHAPTER 19: Broadcast Station

1. Erin Blakemore, "Buzz Aldrin Took Holy Communion on the Moon. NASA Kept It Quiet," History.com, September 6, 2019, www.history.com/news/buzz-aldrin-communion-apollo-11-nasa.
2. "Apollo 11 Mission Overview," NASA, www.nasa.gov/mission_pages/apollo/missions/apollo11.html.

EPILOGUE

1. *Jaws,* directed by Steven Spielberg (Universal City, CA: Universal Pictures, 1975).

BRYAN CRUM was born to a meager upbringing in a log cabin on the banks of the . . . kidding.

By now you know he wrote a children's book banned for using two "bad" words. He's roller-skated through a typhoon using a garbage bag as a sail and once electrocuted his sister with his favorite Christmas present.

Bryan began his career as a hospice chaplain in southeast Ohio. He's spent years helping people reflect on life, confront their mortality, and embrace the Savior who is waiting for all of us with open arms.

Bryan believes we all have stories with sweet, tragic, funny, and profoundly moving parts that we live out. We have stories to be heard, stories to understand, stories to finish well, and Bryan has spent much of his career helping people recognize the brilliant parts of their stories.

Bryan is the guy who brings along a flashlight as people tell their stories. He wants to spotlight the actual words written in bold on our inner framework by our Creator, words that somehow have been forgotten and gone unnoticed. God has written big words inside us, etched them deeply into our being, and printed them in blood because words like *forgiven and loved by our Creator* are our real bios.

Bryan is a military brat who has lived all over the world, and he loves to travel, speak, and entertain crowds.

Bryan lives in Sunbury, Ohio, with his wife and daughter and is a member of Westerville Christian Church. He is a longtime listener, a forever storyteller, and a writer shining a light on our internal design.

Bryan has a bachelor's degree in biblical studies, an MBA from ITT Technical Institute, and certifications from Harvard University in reproductive bioethics and world health, but he says the most important things he's learned have come while sitting at the bedside of people who are dying.

ABOUT THE TYPE

This book was set in Caledonia, a typeface designed in 1939 by W. A. Dwiggins (1880–1956) for the Mergenthaler Linotype Company. Its name is the ancient Roman term for Scotland, because the face was intended to have a Scottish-Roman flavor. Caledonia is considered to be a well-proportioned, businesslike face with little contrast between its thick and thin lines.